A PRAYER GUIDE FOR ADVENT

*Compiled and with an Introduction by
Daniel Lukas*

†
as in heaven
so on earth

©2017 Daniel Lukas
©2017 Lord Teach Us To Pray/As In Heaven So On Earth

-

Psalms updated from ASV

-

Art & Layout By Stephanie Kiel

-

Image by Fr. Ted Bobosh
Licensed Under Creative Commons
Attribution-Share Alike License
Link: creativecommons.org/licenses/by-sa/2.0/

Thank you to:

Stephanie Kiel
Peg Benson
Carol Jorgensen
Melissa Borner
Lane Cross
Lauren Pareigat
Kate Peck
Cassie LaFollette

For their eyes, talent and time.

CONTENTS

An Introduction to This Guide *i*
How to Use This Guide *iv*
Structure *v*
Canticles *vi*

Week One *1*

Week Two *39*

Week Three *79*

Week Four *115*

Christmas Eve Christmastide *153*

AN INTRODUCTION TO THIS GUIDE

The Church Calendar helps us orient our lives around Jesus the Messiah and God's redemptive action in our world; it pulls us into into Sacred Time. Instead of marking time with events like the Olympics or the 4th of July we mark it by remembering God's faithfulness.

The Church Calendar begins with Advent. Here we wait and remember God's faithfulness, we anticipate God's coming. Advent helps us create space to arrive at the great feast of Christmastide where we remember for twelve days Emmanuel, God with us. Christmas is not a feast of one day, but of twelve! God chooses to work through, not around humanity.

Luke tells the story of Jesus' birth with the songs of those who participated in this anticipated moment. As if to say to us his readers, words alone fail and only songs can soar to the heights of telling the beginning of this story. We'll be using those four songs, or canticles, to guide us in prayer through Advent. It's worth noting that that these four canticles actually pre-date the birth of Christ because these prayers echo the prayers of the Torah, the Psalms and the Prophets.

I'm hopeful that this guide might help you cultivate a habit of prayer in your life. The discovery and use of "fixed" prayer — that is, praying prescribed words at specific times — was a significant season of growth in my life. On the following pages is a form, an order, a liturgy for use in prayer. The liturgy prescribes words to begin with, words that Jesus said and knew, words and prayers that formed him. Trustworthy words. These words provide us a good and safe place to cultivate prayer in our lives.

Below is some direction to help as you begin.

The structure of this prayer guide is meant to guide, not restrict. When the liturgy ceases to be helpful, of course it can be set aside. For example, when a line in a prayer stirs something in your soul, you would do well to stop and express what's there: love, frustration, fear. Let scripture, words described as God-breathed, breathe life into you. Those stirrings may just be God's Spirit speaking.

Finishing the prayer form each time is not the goal. The goal is to listen for God. If you complete the prayer liturgy without praying, it was just a liturgy, an ordering of words. That said, part of the potency is the discipline or the habit of doing this very important thing even when you don't feel like it, or when you don't feel rewarded.

If you find yourself with words that do not fit your current mood, consider all these as acceptable alternatives: Pray the words on behalf of someone for whom they might be appropriate. Pray them as preparation for what you may need later. Pray them anyway, noting that your mood should dictate less of what you do.

Many things in life offer us immediate gratification; our lives are virtually instantaneous. In contrast, the work of prayer is frequently slow. These words from Pierre Teilhard de Chardin are apt: "Above all, trust in the slow work of God. We are quite naturally impatient in everything to reach the end without delay,"

When it comes to prayer, we are always students. Let it be your aim to grow, not master. I've found that prayer is best approached as a mystery to be explored. The Lord's Prayer, the Psalms, the Canticles help us nurture a faithful way to prayer.

Prayer is mostly difficult, hidden work. Do not be hard on yourself.

Praying in community is valuable because of prayer's nature as a mostly difficult and hidden work. Perhaps part of your struggle to pray alone is that we are not meant to.

Some of the first signs of change you might perceive within yourself include a more generous spirit, patience, trust, a quelling of fear or anger, and new purpose.

Sometimes the pace of change is too slow for us to perceive; we may be unable to see ourselves growing toward heaven. It can be helpful to have a friend on the way. Community in prayer is helpful.

It critical to remember that to pray is also to listen.

Most of all, consider that your greatest aim in prayer is to be become more like your Maker.

Almost 2000 years ago, one of Jesus' disciples asked a good question that reverberates to this very moment. Let their question and prayer, be ours: Lord, teach us to pray. And as we learn, let us find ourselves living into that great prayer, as in heaven, so on earth.

Daniel Lukas
All Saints Day 2017

HOW TO USE THIS GUIDE

Each day and each portion of each day is completely self-contained. You only have to work your way through the guide as you would read a book; the guide does not require you to page back and forth, pick a prayer or have any existing experience. Everything you need is provided, in order. As you'll see on the following page, the order of the prayer itself is both simple and redundant. This is by design. The core prayers of this guide will have, by the end of Advent become well-worn paths. The experience is meant to form your heart, memory and time to the voice of Scripture.

While this guide can be used at any time, it was made specifically for use during the season of Advent. Day one of the guide is the first day of Advent each year. Each of those days is a Sunday.

Below are where Advent begins over the next seven years.

2017 | December 3
2018 | December 2
2019 | December 1
2020 | November 29
2021 | November 28
2022 | November 27
2023 | December 3

Audio versions of the morning prayers are availabe on the "As In Heaven So On Earth" podcast availabe on Podbean and iTunes.

STRUCTURE FOR THIS PRAYER GUIDE

Morning Prayer
- ☐ Refrain taken from the Canticle for the Week
- ☐ † Silence
- ☐ Canticle for the Week
- ☐ † Silence
- ☐ Refrain taken from the Canticle for the Week
- ☐ Psalm portion
- ☐ Refrain taken from the Canticle for the Week
- ☐ Lord's Prayer
- ☐ Shema & Jesus Creed
- ☐ Closing

Noon Prayer
- ☐ Refrain taken from the Canticle for the Week
- ☐ † Silence
- ☐ Lord's Prayer
- ☐ Shema & Jesus Creed
- ☐ Closing

Evening Prayer
- ☐ Refrain taken from the Canticle for the Week
- ☐ † Silence
- ☐ Canticle for the week with Refrain
- ☐ † Silence
- ☐ Refrain taken from the Canticle for the Week
- ☐ Psalm portion
- ☐ Refrain taken from the Canticle for the Week
- ☐ Lord's Prayer
- ☐ Shema & Jesus Creed
- ☐ Closing

A Prayer Guide for Advent

THE CANTICLES

THE MAGNIFICAT, OR MARY'S SONG
Luke 1:46-55

My soul magnifies the Lord.
My spirit has rejoiced in God my Savior,
For he has looked
At the humble state of his servant.
For behold, from now on,
All generations will call me blessed.
For he who is mighty has done great things for me.
Holy is his name.
His mercy is for generations of generations
On those who fear him.
He has shown strength with his arm.
He has scattered the proud
In the imagination of their hearts.
He has put down princes from their thrones.
And has exalted the lowly.
He has filled the hungry with good things.
He has sent the rich away empty.
He has given help to Israel, his servant,
That he might remember mercy,
As he spoke to our fathers,
To Abraham and his offspring forever.

THE BENEDICTUS, OR ZECHARIAH'S SONG
Luke 1:67-79

Blessed be the Lord,
The God of Israel,
For he has visited
And worked redemption for his people,
And has raised up a horn of salvation for us
In the house of his servant David
As he spoke by the mouth of his holy prophets
That have been from old,
Salvation from our enemies,

And from the hand of all that hate us;
To show mercy towards our fathers,
And to remember his holy covenant;
The oath which he swore to Abraham, our father,
To grant to us, that we being delivered
Out of the Hand of our enemies
Should serve him without fear,
In holiness and righteousness
Before him all our days.
Yea and you, child,
Will be called the prophet of the Most High:
For you will go before the face of the Lord
To prepare his ways;
To give knowledge of salvation to his people
In the forgiveness of their sins,
Because of the tender mercy of our God,
Whereby the dayspring from on high will visit us,
To shine upon them that sit
In darkness and the shadow of death;
To guide our feet into the way of peace.

THE GLORIA, OR THE ANGEL'S SONG
Luke 2:9-14

Glory to God in the highest heavens,
And on earth peace
Among men in whom he is well pleased.

THE NUNC DIMITTIS, OR SIMEON AND ANNA'S SONG
Luke 2:28-32

Now let your servant depart, Lord
According to your word,
In peace
For my eyes have seen your salvation,
Which you prepared
Before the face of all peoples;
A light for revelation to the Gentiles,
And the glory of your people Israel.
To Abraham and his offspring forever.

A PRAYER GUIDE FOR ADVENT
WEEK ONE

DAY 1
MORNING
—

REFRAIN
That he might remember mercy.

† SILENCE

THE MAGNIFICAT
My soul magnifies the Lord.
My spirit has rejoiced in God my Savior,
For he has looked
At the humble state of his servant.
For behold, from now on,
All generations will call me blessed.
For he who is mighty has done great things for me.
Holy is his name.
His mercy is for generations of generations
On those who fear him.
He has shown strength with his arm.
He has scattered the proud
In the imagination of their hearts.
He has put down princes from their thrones.
And has exalted the lowly.
He has filled the hungry with good things.
He has sent the rich away empty.
He has given help to Israel, his servant,
That he might remember mercy,
As he spoke to our fathers,
To Abraham and his offspring forever.

† SILENCE

REFRAIN
That he might remember mercy.

PSALM 34
Yahweh is near to the broken heart,
And saves those crushed in spirit.
Many are the afflictions of the righteous;
But Yahweh delivers them out of them all.

REFRAIN
That he might remember mercy.

THE LORD'S PRAYER
Our Father in heaven
Hallowed be your name
Your kingdom come
Your will be done
On earth as it is in heaven
Give us this day our daily bread
Forgive us our debts as we forgive our debtors
Lead us not into temptation
But deliver us from the evil one
For yours is the kingdom and the power and the glory
Forever and ever

SHEMA & THE JESUS CREED
Hear, O Israel:
The Lord is our God, the Lord alone. You shall love the Lord your God with all your heart, and with all your soul and with all your might. You shall love your neighbor as yourself. There is no commandment greater than these.

CLOSING
We say yes! Amen!
Come Lord Jesus.

DAY 1
NOON
—

REFRAIN
That he might remember mercy.

† SILENCE

THE LORD'S PRAYER
Our Father in heaven
Hallowed be your name
Your kingdom come
Your will be done
On earth as it is in heaven
Give us this day our daily bread
Forgive us our debts as we forgive our debtors
Lead us not into temptation
But deliver us from the evil one
For yours is the kingdom and the power and the glory
Forever and ever

SHEMA & THE JESUS CREED
Hear, O Israel:
The Lord is our God, the Lord alone. You shall love the Lord your God with all your heart, and with all your soul and with all your might. You shall love your neighbor as yourself. There is no commandment greater than these.

CLOSING
We say yes! Amen!
Come Lord Jesus.

DAY 1
EVENING
—

REFRAIN
That he might remember mercy.

† SILENCE

THE MAGNIFICAT
My soul magnifies the Lord.
My spirit has rejoiced in God my Savior,
For he has looked
At the humble state of his servant.

That he might remember mercy.

For behold, from now on,
All generations will call me blessed.
For he who is mighty has done great things for me.
Holy is his name.
His mercy is for generations of generations
On those who fear him.

That he might remember mercy.

He has shown strength with his arm.
He has scattered the proud
In the imagination of their hearts.
He has put down princes from their thrones.
And has exalted the lowly.
He has filled the hungry with good things.
He has sent the rich away empty.
He has given help to Israel, his servant,
That he might remember mercy,
As he spoke to our fathers,
To Abraham and his offspring forever.

† SILENCE

REFRAIN
That he might remember mercy.

PSALM 54
Save me, O God, by your name,
And judge me in your might.
Hear my prayer, O God;
Give ear to the words of my mouth.
Behold, God is my helper:
The Lord is of those that uphold my soul.

REFRAIN
That he might remember mercy.

THE LORD'S PRAYER
Our Father in heaven
Hallowed be your name
Your kingdom come
Your will be done
On earth as it is in heaven
Give us this day our daily bread
Forgive us our debts as we forgive our debtors
Lead us not into temptation
But deliver us from the evil one
For yours is the kingdom and the power and the glory
Forever and ever

SHEMA & THE JESUS CREED
Hear, O Israel:
The Lord is our God, the Lord alone. You shall love the Lord your God with all your heart, and with all your soul and with all your might. You shall love your neighbor as yourself. There is no commandment greater than these.

CLOSING
We say yes! Amen!
Come Lord Jesus.

DAY 2
MORNING

—

REFRAIN
He who is mighty.

† SILENCE

THE MAGNIFICAT
My soul magnifies the Lord.
My spirit has rejoiced in God my Savior,
For he has looked
At the humble state of his servant.
For behold, from now on,
All generations will call me blessed.
For he who is mighty has done great things for me.
Holy is his name.
His mercy is for generations of generations
On those who fear him.
He has shown strength with his arm.
He has scattered the proud
In the imagination of their hearts.
He has put down princes from their thrones.
And has exalted the lowly.
He has filled the hungry with good things.
He has sent the rich away empty.
He has given help to Israel, his servant,
That he might remember mercy,
As he spoke to our fathers,
To Abraham and his offspring forever.

† SILENCE

REFRAIN
He who is mighty.

PSALM 28

Yahweh is their strength,
And he is a stronghold of salvation to his anointed.
Save your people, and bless your inheritance:
Be their shepherd also, and bear them up forever.

REFRAIN

He who is mighty.

THE LORD'S PRAYER

Our Father in heaven
Hallowed be your name
Your kingdom come
Your will be done
On earth as it is in heaven
Give us this day our daily bread
Forgive us our debts as we forgive our debtors
Lead us not into temptation
But deliver us from the evil one
For yours is the kingdom and the power and the glory
Forever and ever

SHEMA & THE JESUS CREED

Hear, O Israel:
The Lord is our God, the Lord alone. You shall love the Lord your God with all your heart, and with all your soul and with all your might. You shall love your neighbor as yourself. There is no commandment greater than these.

CLOSING

We say yes! Amen!
Come Lord Jesus.

DAY 2
NOON

REFRAIN
He who is mighty.

† SILENCE

THE LORD'S PRAYER
Our Father in heaven
Hallowed be your name
Your kingdom come
Your will be done
On earth as it is in heaven
Give us this day our daily bread
Forgive us our debts as we forgive our debtors
Lead us not into temptation
But deliver us from the evil one
For yours is the kingdom and the power and the glory
Forever and ever

SHEMA & THE JESUS CREED
Hear, O Israel:
The Lord is our God, the Lord alone. You shall love the Lord your God with all your heart, and with all your soul and with all your might. You shall love your neighbor as yourself. There is no commandment greater than these.

CLOSING
We say yes! Amen!
Come Lord Jesus.

DAY 2
EVENING
—

REFRAIN
He who is mighty.

† SILENCE

THE MAGNIFICAT
My soul magnifies the Lord.
My spirit has rejoiced in God my Savior,
For he has looked
At the humble state of his servant.
For behold, from now on,
All generations will call me blessed.
For he who is mighty has done great things for me.
Holy is his name.
His mercy is for generations of generations
On those who fear him.
He has shown strength with his arm.
He has scattered the proud
In the imagination of their hearts.

He who is mighty.

He has put down princes from their thrones.
And has exalted the lowly.
He has filled the hungry with good things.
He has sent the rich away empty.

He who is mighty.

He has given help to Israel, his servant,
That he might remember mercy,
As he spoke to our fathers,
To Abraham and his offspring forever.

He who is mighty.

† SILENCE

A Prayer Guide for Advent

REFRAIN
He who is mighty.

PSALM 24
Who is the King of glory?
Yahweh strong and mighty,
Yahweh mighty in battle.

REFRAIN
He who is mighty.

THE LORD'S PRAYER
Our Father in heaven
Hallowed be your name
Your kingdom come
Your will be done
On earth as it is in heaven
Give us this day our daily bread
Forgive us our debts as we forgive our debtors
Lead us not into temptation
But deliver us from the evil one
For yours is the kingdom and the power and the glory
Forever and ever

SHEMA & THE JESUS CREED
Hear, O Israel:
The Lord is our God, the Lord alone. You shall love the Lord your God with all your heart, and with all your soul and with all your might. You shall love your neighbor as yourself. There is no commandment greater than these.

CLOSING
We say yes! Amen!
Come Lord Jesus.

DAY 3
MORNING

—

REFRAIN
God my Savior.

† SILENCE

THE MAGNIFICAT
My soul magnifies the Lord.
My spirit has rejoiced in God my Savior,
For he has looked
At the humble state of his servant.
For behold, from now on,
All generations will call me blessed.
For he who is mighty has done great things for me.
Holy is his name.
His mercy is for generations of generations
On those who fear him.
He has shown strength with his arm.
He has scattered the proud
In the imagination of their hearts.
He has put down princes from their thrones.
And has exalted the lowly.
He has filled the hungry with good things.
He has sent the rich away empty.
He has given help to Israel, his servant,
That he might remember mercy,
As he spoke to our fathers,
To Abraham and his offspring forever.

† SILENCE

REFRAIN
God my Savior.

PSALM 122
I was glad when they said to me,
Let us go to the house of Yahweh.
Our feet are standing
Within your gates, O Jerusalem.

REFRAIN
God my Savior.

THE LORD'S PRAYER
Our Father in heaven
Hallowed be your name
Your kingdom come
Your will be done
On earth as it is in heaven
Give us this day our daily bread
Forgive us our debts as we forgive our debtors
Lead us not into temptation
But deliver us from the evil one
For yours is the kingdom and the power and the glory
Forever and ever

SHEMA & THE JESUS CREED
Hear, O Israel:
The Lord is our God, the Lord alone. You shall love the Lord your God with all your heart, and with all your soul and with all your might. You shall love your neighbor as yourself. There is no commandment greater than these.

CLOSING
We say yes! Amen!
Come Lord Jesus.

DAY 3
NOON

—

REFRAIN
God my Savior.

† SILENCE

THE LORD'S PRAYER
Our Father in heaven
Hallowed be your name
Your kingdom come
Your will be done
On earth as it is in heaven
Give us this day our daily bread
Forgive us our debts as we forgive our debtors
Lead us not into temptation
But deliver us from the evil one
For yours is the kingdom and the power and the glory
Forever and ever

SHEMA & THE JESUS CREED
Hear, O Israel:
The Lord is our God, the Lord alone. You shall love the Lord your God with all your heart, and with all your soul and with all your might. You shall love your neighbor as yourself. There is no commandment greater than these.

CLOSING
We say yes! Amen!
Come Lord Jesus.

DAY 3
EVENING

—

REFRAIN
God my Savior.

† SILENCE

THE MAGNIFICAT
My soul magnifies the Lord.
My spirit has rejoiced in God my Savior,
For he has looked
At the humble state of his servant.
For behold, from now on,
All generations will call me blessed.
For he who is mighty has done great things for me.
Holy is his name.

God my Savior.

His mercy is for generations of generations
On those who fear him.
He has shown strength with his arm.
He has scattered the proud
In the imagination of their hearts.

God my Savior.

He has put down princes from their thrones.
And has exalted the lowly.
He has filled the hungry with good things.
He has sent the rich away empty.
He has given help to Israel, his servant,
That he might remember mercy,
As he spoke to our fathers,
To Abraham and his offspring forever.

God my Savior.

† SILENCE

REFRAIN
God my Savior.

PSALM 113
Praise the name of Yahweh.
Blessed be the name of Yahweh
From this time forth and forevermore.
From the rising of the sun
Unto the going down of the same
Yahweh's name is to be praised.

REFRAIN
God my Savior.

THE LORD'S PRAYER
Our Father in heaven
Hallowed be your name
Your kingdom come
Your will be done
On earth as it is in heaven
Give us this day our daily bread
Forgive us our debts as we forgive our debtors
Lead us not into temptation
But deliver us from the evil one
For yours is the kingdom and the power and the glory
Forever and ever

SHEMA & THE JESUS CREED
Hear, O Israel:
The Lord is our God, the Lord alone. You shall love the Lord your God with all your heart, and with all your soul and with all your might. You shall love your neighbor as yourself. There is no commandment greater than these.

CLOSING
We say yes! Amen!
Come Lord Jesus.

DAY 4
MORNING
—

REFRAIN
He has filled the hungry.

† SILENCE

THE MAGNIFICAT
My soul magnifies the Lord.
My spirit has rejoiced in God my Savior,
For he has looked
At the humble state of his servant.
For behold, from now on,
All generations will call me blessed.
For he who is mighty has done great things for me.
Holy is his name.
His mercy is for generations of generations
On those who fear him.
He has shown strength with his arm.
He has scattered the proud
In the imagination of their hearts.
He has put down princes from their thrones.
And has exalted the lowly.
He has filled the hungry with good things.
He has sent the rich away empty.
He has given help to Israel, his servant,
That he might remember mercy,
As he spoke to our fathers,
To Abraham and his offspring forever.

† SILENCE

REFRAIN
He has filled the hungry.

PSALM 130
I wait for Yahweh, my soul does wait,
And in his word do I hope.

My soul waits for the Lord
More than watchmen wait for the morning;
Yea, more than watchmen for the morning.

REFRAIN
He has filled the hungry.

THE LORD'S PRAYER
Our Father in heaven
Hallowed be your name
Your kingdom come
Your will be done
On earth as it is in heaven
Give us this day our daily bread
Forgive us our debts as we forgive our debtors
Lead us not into temptation
But deliver us from the evil one
For yours is the kingdom and the power and the glory
Forever and ever

SHEMA & THE JESUS CREED
Hear, O Israel:
The Lord is our God, the Lord alone. You shall love the Lord your God with all your heart, and with all your soul and with all your might. You shall love your neighbor as yourself. There is no commandment greater than these.

CLOSING
We say yes! Amen!
Come Lord Jesus.

DAY 4
NOON
—

REFRAIN
He has filled the hungry.

† SILENCE

THE LORD'S PRAYER
Our Father in heaven
Hallowed be your name
Your kingdom come
Your will be done
On earth as it is in heaven
Give us this day our daily bread
Forgive us our debts as we forgive our debtors
Lead us not into temptation
But deliver us from the evil one
For yours is the kingdom and the power and the glory
Forever and ever

SHEMA & THE JESUS CREED
Hear, O Israel:
The Lord is our God, the Lord alone. You shall love the Lord your God with all your heart, and with all your soul and with all your might. You shall love your neighbor as yourself. There is no commandment greater than these.

CLOSING
We say yes! Amen!
Come Lord Jesus.

DAY 4
EVENING
—

REFRAIN
He has filled the hungry.

† SILENCE

THE MAGNIFICAT
He has filled the hungry.

My soul magnifies the Lord.
My spirit has rejoiced in God my Savior,
For he has looked
At the humble state of his servant.

For behold, from now on,
All generations will call me blessed.
For he who is mighty has done great things for me.
Holy is his name.
His mercy is for generations of generations
On those who fear him.

He has filled the hungry.

He has shown strength with his arm.
He has scattered the proud
In the imagination of their hearts.
He has put down princes from their thrones.
And has exalted the lowly.
He has filled the hungry with good things.
He has sent the rich away empty.
He has given help to Israel, his servant,
That he might remember mercy,
As he spoke to our fathers,
To Abraham and his offspring forever.

He has filled the hungry.

† SILENCE

REFRAIN
He has filled the hungry.

PSALM 119
For you have taught me.
How sweet are your words unto my taste!
Yea, sweeter than honey to my mouth!

REFRAIN
He has filled the hungry.

THE LORD'S PRAYER
Our Father in heaven
Hallowed be your name
Your kingdom come

Your will be done
On earth as it is in heaven
Give us this day our daily bread
Forgive us our debts as we forgive our debtors
Lead us not into temptation
But deliver us from the evil one
For yours is the kingdom and the power and the glory
Forever and ever

SHEMA & THE JESUS CREED
Hear, O Israel:
The Lord is our God, the Lord alone. You shall love the Lord your God with all your heart, and with all your soul and with all your might. You shall love your neighbor as yourself. There is no commandment greater than these.

CLOSING
We say yes! Amen!
Come Lord Jesus.

DAY 5
MORNING
—

REFRAIN
As he spoke to our fathers.

† SILENCE

THE MAGNIFICAT
My soul magnifies the Lord.
My spirit has rejoiced in God my Savior,
For he has looked
At the humble state of his servant.
For behold, from now on,
All generations will call me blessed.
For he who is mighty has done great things for me.
Holy is his name.
His mercy is for generations of generations
On those who fear him.
He has shown strength with his arm.
He has scattered the proud
In the imagination of their hearts.
He has put down princes from their thrones.
And has exalted the lowly.
He has filled the hungry with good things.
He has sent the rich away empty.
He has given help to Israel, his servant,
That he might remember mercy,
As he spoke to our fathers,
To Abraham and his offspring forever.

† SILENCE

REFRAIN
As he spoke to our fathers.

PSALM 1
Blessed is the man that walks
Not in the counsel of the wicked,
Nor stands in the way of sinners,

Nor sits in the seat of scoffers:
But his delight is in the law of Yahweh;
And on his law he meditates day and night.

REFRAIN
As he spoke to our fathers.

THE LORD'S PRAYER
Our Father in heaven
Hallowed be your name
Your kingdom come
Your will be done
On earth as it is in heaven
Give us this day our daily bread
Forgive us our debts as we forgive our debtors
Lead us not into temptation
But deliver us from the evil one
For yours is the kingdom and the power and the glory
Forever and ever

SHEMA & THE JESUS CREED
Hear, O Israel:
The Lord is our God, the Lord alone. You shall love the Lord your God with all your heart, and with all your soul and with all your might. You shall love your neighbor as yourself. There is no commandment greater than these.

CLOSING
We say yes! Amen!
Come Lord Jesus.

DAY 5
NOON
—

REFRAIN
As he spoke to our fathers.

† SILENCE

THE LORD'S PRAYER
Our Father in heaven
Hallowed be your name
Your kingdom come
Your will be done
On earth as it is in heaven
Give us this day our daily bread
Forgive us our debts as we forgive our debtors
Lead us not into temptation
But deliver us from the evil one
For yours is the kingdom and the power and the glory
Forever and ever

SHEMA & THE JESUS CREED
Hear, O Israel:
The Lord is our God, the Lord alone. You shall love the Lord your God with all your heart, and with all your soul and with all your might. You shall love your neighbor as yourself. There is no commandment greater than these.

CLOSING
We say yes! Amen!
Come Lord Jesus.

DAY 5
EVENING
—

REFRAIN
As he spoke to our fathers.

† SILENCE

THE MAGNIFICAT
As he spoke to our fathers.

My soul magnifies the Lord.
My spirit has rejoiced in God my Savior,
For he has looked
At the humble state of his servant.

For behold, from now on,
All generations will call me blessed.
For he who is mighty has done great things for me.
Holy is his name.
His mercy is for generations of generations
On those who fear him.
He has shown strength with his arm.
He has scattered the proud
In the imagination of their hearts.

As he spoke to our fathers.

He has put down princes from their thrones.
And has exalted the lowly.
He has filled the hungry with good things.
He has sent the rich away empty.
He has given help to Israel, his servant,
That he might remember mercy,
As he spoke to our fathers,
To Abraham and his offspring forever.

As he spoke to our fathers.

✝ SILENCE

REFRAIN
As he spoke to our fathers.

PSALM 119
Your word have I laid up in my heart,
That I might not sin against you.
Blessed are you, O Yahweh:
Teach me your statutes.

REFRAIN
As he spoke to our fathers.

THE LORD'S PRAYER
Our Father in heaven
Hallowed be your name

Your kingdom come
Your will be done
On earth as it is in heaven
Give us this day our daily bread
Forgive us our debts as we forgive our debtors
Lead us not into temptation
But deliver us from the evil one
For yours is the kingdom and the power and the glory
Forever and ever

SHEMA & THE JESUS CREED
Hear, O Israel:
The Lord is our God, the Lord alone. You shall love the Lord your God with all your heart, and with all your soul and with all your might. You shall love your neighbor as yourself. There is no commandment greater than these.

CLOSING
We say yes! Amen!
Come Lord Jesus.

DAY 6
MORNING
—

REFRAIN
For he has looked.

† SILENCE

THE MAGNIFICAT
My soul magnifies the Lord.
My spirit has rejoiced in God my Savior,
For he has looked
At the humble state of his servant.
For behold, from now on,
All generations will call me blessed.
For he who is mighty has done great things for me.
Holy is his name.
His mercy is for generations of generations
On those who fear him.
He has shown strength with his arm.
He has scattered the proud
In the imagination of their hearts.
He has put down princes from their thrones.
And has exalted the lowly.
He has filled the hungry with good things.
He has sent the rich away empty.
He has given help to Israel, his servant,
That he might remember mercy,
As he spoke to our fathers,
To Abraham and his offspring forever.

† SILENCE

REFRAIN
For he has looked.

PSALM 117
Praise Yahweh, all you nations;
Laud him, all peoples.
For his lovingkindness is great toward us;

And the truth of Yahweh endures forever.
Praise Yahweh.

REFRAIN
For he has looked.

THE LORD'S PRAYER
Our Father in heaven
Hallowed be your name
Your kingdom come
Your will be done
On earth as it is in heaven
Give us this day our daily bread
Forgive us our debts as we forgive our debtors
Lead us not into temptation
But deliver us from the evil one
For yours is the kingdom and the power and the glory
Forever and ever

SHEMA & THE JESUS CREED
Hear, O Israel:
The Lord is our God, the Lord alone. You shall love the Lord your God with all your heart, and with all your soul and with all your might. You shall love your neighbor as yourself. There is no commandment greater than these.

CLOSING
We say yes! Amen!
Come Lord Jesus.

DAY 6
NOON
—

REFRAIN
For he has looked.

† SILENCE

THE LORD'S PRAYER
Our Father in heaven
Hallowed be your name
Your kingdom come
Your will be done
On earth as it is in heaven
Give us this day our daily bread
Forgive us our debts as we forgive our debtors
Lead us not into temptation
But deliver us from the evil one
For yours is the kingdom and the power and the glory
Forever and ever

SHEMA & THE JESUS CREED
Hear, O Israel:
The Lord is our God, the Lord alone. You shall love the Lord your God with all your heart, and with all your soul and with all your might. You shall love your neighbor as yourself. There is no commandment greater than these.

CLOSING
We say yes! Amen!
Come Lord Jesus.

DAY 6
EVENING
—

REFRAIN
For he has looked.

† SILENCE

THE MAGNIFICAT
For he has looked.

My soul magnifies the Lord.
My spirit has rejoiced in God my Savior,

For he has looked
At the humble state of his servant.
For behold, from now on,
All generations will call me blessed.

For he has looked.

For he who is mighty has done great things for me.
Holy is his name.
His mercy is for generations of generations
On those who fear him.

For he has looked.

He has shown strength with his arm.
He has scattered the proud
In the imagination of their hearts.
He has put down princes from their thrones.
And has exalted the lowly.
He has filled the hungry with good things.
He has sent the rich away empty.

For he has looked.

He has given help to Israel, his servant,
That he might remember mercy,
As he spoke to our fathers,
To Abraham and his offspring forever.

† SILENCE

REFRAIN
For he has looked.

PSALM 6
I am weary with my groaning;
Every night I make my bed to swim;
I water my couch with my tears.
My eyes no longer work because of grief;
They grow old because of all my enemies.

Depart from me, all who work iniquity;
Yahweh has heard the voice of my weeping.

REFRAIN
For he has looked.

THE LORD'S PRAYER
Our Father in heaven
Hallowed be your name
Your kingdom come
Your will be done
On earth as it is in heaven
Give us this day our daily bread
Forgive us our debts as we forgive our debtors
Lead us not into temptation
But deliver us from the evil one
For yours is the kingdom and the power and the glory
Forever and ever

SHEMA & THE JESUS CREED
Hear, O Israel:
The Lord is our God, the Lord alone. You shall love the Lord your God with all your heart, and with all your soul and with all your might. You shall love your neighbor as yourself. There is no commandment greater than these.

CLOSING
We say yes! Amen!
Come Lord Jesus.

DAY 7
MORNING
—

REFRAIN
He has given help.

† SILENCE

THE MAGNIFICAT
My soul magnifies the Lord.
My spirit has rejoiced in God my Savior,
For he has looked at the humble state of his servant.
For behold, from now on,
All generations will call me blessed.
For he who is mighty has done great things for me.
Holy is his name.
His mercy is for generations of generations
On those who fear him.
He has shown strength with his arm.
He has scattered the proud
In the imagination of their hearts.
He has put down princes from their thrones.
And has exalted the lowly.
He has filled the hungry with good things.
He has sent the rich away empty.
He has given help to Israel, his servant,
That he might remember mercy,
As he spoke to our fathers,
To Abraham and his offspring forever.

† SILENCE

REFRAIN
He has given help.

PSALM 28
He rescues me from my enemies;
Yea, you lift me up
Above those who rise up against me;
You deliver me from the violent man.

REFRAIN
He has given help.

THE LORD'S PRAYER
Our Father in heaven
Hallowed be your name
Your kingdom come
Your will be done
On earth as it is in heaven
Give us this day our daily bread
Forgive us our debts as we forgive our debtors
Lead us not into temptation
But deliver us from the evil one
For yours is the kingdom and the power and the glory
Forever and ever

SHEMA & THE JESUS CREED
Hear, O Israel:
The Lord is our God, the Lord alone. You shall love the Lord your God with all your heart, and with all your soul and with all your might. You shall love your neighbor as yourself. There is no commandment greater than these.

CLOSING
We say yes! Amen!
Come Lord Jesus.

DAY 7
NOON
—

REFRAIN
He has given help.

† SILENCE

THE LORD'S PRAYER
Our Father in heaven
Hallowed be your name

Your kingdom come
Your will be done
On earth as it is in heaven
Give us this day our daily bread
Forgive us our debts as we forgive our debtors
Lead us not into temptation
But deliver us from the evil one
For yours is the kingdom and the power and the glory
Forever and ever

SHEMA & THE JESUS CREED
Hear, O Israel:
The Lord is our God, the Lord alone. You shall love the Lord your God with all your heart, and with all your soul and with all your might. You shall love your neighbor as yourself. There is no commandment greater than these.

CLOSING
We say yes! Amen!
Come Lord Jesus.

DAY 7
EVENING
—

REFRAIN
He has given help.

† SILENCE

THE MAGNIFICAT
He has given help.

My soul magnifies the Lord.
My spirit has rejoiced in God my Savior,
For he has looked
At the humble state of his servant.
For behold, from now on,
All generations will call me blessed.

He has given help.

For he who is mighty has done great things for me.
Holy is his name.
His mercy is for generations of generations
On those who fear him.
He has shown strength with his arm.
He has scattered the proud
In the imagination of their hearts.

He has given help.

He has put down princes from their thrones.
And has exalted the lowly.
He has filled the hungry with good things.
He has sent the rich away empty.
He has given help to Israel, his servant,
That he might remember mercy,
As he spoke to our fathers,
To Abraham and his offspring forever.

He has given help.

† SILENCE

REFRAIN
He has given help.

PSALM 146
While I live will I praise Yahweh:
I will sing praises unto my God while I have any being.
Do not put your trust in princes,
Nor in the son of man, in whom there is no help.

REFRAIN
He has given help.

THE LORD'S PRAYER
Our Father in heaven
Hallowed be your name

Your kingdom come
Your will be done
On earth as it is in heaven
Give us this day our daily bread
Forgive us our debts as we forgive our debtors
Lead us not into temptation
But deliver us from the evil one
For yours is the kingdom and the power and the glory
Forever and ever

SHEMA & THE JESUS CREED
Hear, O Israel:
The Lord is our God, the Lord alone. You shall love the Lord your God with all your heart, and with all your soul and with all your might. You shall love your neighbor as yourself. There is no commandment greater than these.

CLOSING
We say yes! Amen!
Come Lord Jesus.

A PRAYER GUIDE FOR ADVENT
WEEK TWO

DAY 8
MORNING
—

REFRAIN
For he has visited.

† SILENCE

THE BENEDICTUS
Blessed be the Lord,
The God of Israel,
For he has visited
And worked redemption for his people,
And has raised up a horn of salvation for us
In the house of his servant David
As he spoke by the mouth of his holy prophets
That have been from old,
Salvation from our enemies,
And from the hand of all that hate us;
To show mercy towards our fathers,
And to remember his holy covenant;
The oath which he swore to Abraham, our father,
To grant to us, that we being delivered
Out of the hand of our enemies
Should serve him without fear,
In holiness and righteousness
Before him all our days.
Yea and you, child,
Will be called the prophet of the Most High:
For you will go before the face of the Lord
To prepare his ways;
To give knowledge of salvation to his people
In the forgiveness of their sins,
Because of the tender mercy of our God,
Whereby the dayspring from on high will visit us,
To shine upon them that sit
In darkness and the shadow of death;
To guide our feet into the way of peace.

† SILENCE

REFRAIN
For he has visited.

PSALM 80
Turn again, please, God of hosts:
Look down from heaven,
Behold, and visit this vine,
The stock which your right hand planted,
And the branch that you made strong for yourself.

REFRAIN
For he has visited.

THE LORD'S PRAYER
Our Father in heaven
Hallowed be your name
Your kingdom come
Your will be done
On earth as it is in heaven
Give us this day our daily bread
Forgive us our debts as we forgive our debtors
Lead us not into temptation
But deliver us from the evil one
For yours is the kingdom and the power and the glory
Forever and ever

SHEMA & THE JESUS CREED
Hear, O Israel:
The Lord is our God, the Lord alone. You shall love the Lord your God with all your heart, and with all your soul and with all your might. You shall love your neighbor as yourself. There is no commandment greater than these.

CLOSING
We say yes! Amen!
Come Lord Jesus.

DAY 8
NOON

—

REFRAIN
For he has visited.

† SILENCE

THE LORD'S PRAYER
Our Father in heaven
Hallowed be your name
Your kingdom come
Your will be done
On earth as it is in heaven
Give us this day our daily bread
Forgive us our debts as we forgive our debtors
Lead us not into temptation
But deliver us from the evil one
For yours is the kingdom and the power and the glory
Forever and ever

SHEMA & THE JESUS CREED
Hear, O Israel:
The Lord is our God, the Lord alone. You shall love the Lord your God with all your heart, and with all your soul and with all your might. You shall love your neighbor as yourself. There is no commandment greater than these.

CLOSING
We say yes! Amen!
Come Lord Jesus.

DAY 8
EVENING

—

REFRAIN
For he has visited.

† SILENCE

THE BENEDICTUS
For he has visited.

Blessed be the Lord,
The God of Israel,
For he has visited
And worked redemption for his people,
And has raised up a horn of salvation for us
In the house of his servant David
As he spoke by the mouth of his holy prophets
That have been from old,
Salvation from our enemies,
And from the hand of all that hate us;

For he has visited.

To show mercy towards our fathers,
And to remember his holy covenant;
The oath which he swore to Abraham, our father,
To grant to us, that we being delivered
Out of the hand of our enemies
Should serve him without fear,
In holiness and righteousness
Before him all our days.

For he has visited.

Yea and you, child,
Will be called the prophet of the Most High:
For you will go before the face of the Lord
To prepare his ways;
To give knowledge of salvation to his people
In the forgiveness of their sins,

For he has visited.

Because of the tender mercy of our God,
Whereby the dayspring from on high will visit us,
To shine upon them that sit

In darkness and the shadow of death;
To guide our feet into the way of peace.

† SILENCE

REFRAIN
For he has visited.

PSALM 106
Remember me, O Yahweh,
With the favor that you bear unto your people;
Visit me with your salvation.

REFRAIN
For he has visited.

THE LORD'S PRAYER
Our Father in heaven
Hallowed be your name
Your kingdom come
Your will be done
On earth as it is in heaven
Give us this day our daily bread
Forgive us our debts as we forgive our debtors
Lead us not into temptation
But deliver us from the evil one
For yours is the kingdom and the power and the glory
Forever and ever

SHEMA & THE JESUS CREED
Hear, O Israel:
The Lord is our God, the Lord alone. You shall love the Lord
your God with all your heart, and with all your soul and with all
your might. You shall love your neighbor as yourself. There is no
commandment greater than these.

CLOSING
We say yes! Amen!
Come Lord Jesus.

DAY 9
MORNING

—

REFRAIN
Give knowledge of salvation.

† SILENCE

THE BENEDICTUS
Blessed be the Lord,
The God of Israel,
For he has visited
And worked redemption for his people,
And has raised up a horn of salvation for us
In the house of his servant David
As he spoke by the mouth of his holy prophets
That have been from old,
Salvation from our enemies,
And from the hand of all that hate us;
To show mercy towards our fathers,
And to remember his holy covenant;
The oath which he swore to Abraham, our father,
To grant to us, that we being delivered
Out of the hand of our enemies
Should serve him without fear,
In holiness and righteousness
Before him all our days.
Yea and you, child,
Will be called the prophet of the Most High:
For you will go before the face of the Lord
To prepare his ways;
To give knowledge of salvation to his people
In the forgiveness of their sins,
Because of the tender mercy of our God,
Whereby the dayspring from on high will visit us,
To shine upon them that sit
In darkness and the shadow of death;
To guide our feet into the way of peace.

† SILENCE

REFRAIN
Give knowledge of salvation.

PSALM 116
What shall I render unto Yahweh
For all his benefits toward me?
I will take the cup of salvation,
And call upon the name of Yahweh.

REFRAIN
Give knowledge of salvation.

THE LORD'S PRAYER
Our Father in heaven
Hallowed be your name
Your kingdom come
Your will be done
On earth as it is in heaven
Give us this day our daily bread
Forgive us our debts as we forgive our debtors
Lead us not into temptation
But deliver us from the evil one
For yours is the kingdom and the power and the glory
Forever and ever

SHEMA & THE JESUS CREED
Hear, O Israel:
The Lord is our God, the Lord alone. You shall love the Lord your God with all your heart, and with all your soul and with all your might. You shall love your neighbor as yourself. There is no commandment greater than these.

CLOSING
We say yes! Amen!
Come Lord Jesus.

DAY 9
NOON
—

REFRAIN
Give knowledge of salvation.

† SILENCE

THE LORD'S PRAYER
Our Father in heaven
Hallowed be your name
Your kingdom come
Your will be done
On earth as it is in heaven
Give us this day our daily bread
Forgive us our debts as we forgive our debtors
Lead us not into temptation
But deliver us from the evil one
For yours is the kingdom and the power and the glory
Forever and ever

SHEMA & THE JESUS CREED
Hear, O Israel:
The Lord is our God, the Lord alone. You shall love the Lord your God with all your heart, and with all your soul and with all your might. You shall love your neighbor as yourself. There is no commandment greater than these.

CLOSING
We say yes! Amen!
Come Lord Jesus.

DAY 9
EVENING
—

REFRAIN
Give knowledge of salvation.

† SILENCE

THE BENEDICTUS
Give knowledge of salvation.

Blessed be the Lord,
The God of Israel,
For he has visited
And worked redemption for his people,
And has raised up a horn of salvation for us
In the house of his servant David
As he spoke by the mouth of his holy prophets
That have been from old,

Give knowledge of salvation.

Salvation from our enemies,
And from the hand of all that hate us;
To show mercy towards our fathers,
And to remember his holy covenant;
The oath which he swore to Abraham, our father,
To grant to us, that we being delivered
Out of the hand of our enemies
Should serve him without fear,
In holiness and righteousness
Before him all our days.

Give knowledge of salvation.

Yea and you, child,
Will be called the prophet of the Most High:
For you will go before the face of the Lord
To prepare his ways;
To give knowledge of salvation to his people
In the forgiveness of their sins,
Because of the tender mercy of our God,
Whereby the dayspring from on high will visit us,
To shine upon them that sit
In darkness and the shadow of death;
To guide our feet into the way of peace.

† SILENCE

REFRAIN
Give knowledge of salvation.

PSALM 3
Arise, O Yahweh;
Save me, O my God:
For you have struck all my enemies on the cheek;
You have broken the teeth of the wicked.
Salvation belongs to Yahweh:
Your blessing be on your people.

REFRAIN
Give knowledge of salvation.

THE LORD'S PRAYER
Our Father in heaven
Hallowed be your name
Your kingdom come
Your will be done
On earth as it is in heaven
Give us this day our daily bread
Forgive us our debts as we forgive our debtors
Lead us not into temptation
But deliver us from the evil one
For yours is the kingdom and the power and the glory
Forever and ever

SHEMA & THE JESUS CREED
Hear, O Israel:
The Lord is our God, the Lord alone. You shall love the Lord your God with all your heart, and with all your soul and with all your might. You shall love your neighbor as yourself. There is no commandment greater than these.

CLOSING
We say yes! Amen!
Come Lord Jesus.

DAY 10
MORNING
—

REFRAIN
He spoke by the mouth of his holy prophets.

† SILENCE

THE BENEDICTUS
Blessed be the Lord,
The God of Israel,
For he has visited
And worked redemption for his people,
And has raised up a horn of salvation for us
In the house of his servant David
As he spoke by the mouth of his holy prophets
That have been from old,
Salvation from our enemies,
And from the hand of all that hate us;
To show mercy towards our fathers,
And to remember his holy covenant;
The oath which he swore to Abraham, our father,
To grant to us, that we being delivered
Out of the hand of our enemies
Should serve him without fear,
In holiness and righteousness
Before him all our days.
Yea and you, child,
Will be called the prophet of the Most High:
For you will go before the face of the Lord
To prepare his ways;
To give knowledge of salvation to his people
In the forgiveness of their sins,
Because of the tender mercy of our God,
Whereby the dayspring from on high will visit us,
To shine upon them that sit
In darkness and the shadow of death;
To guide our feet into the way of peace.

† SILENCE

REFRAIN
He spoke by the mouth of his holy prophets.

PSALM 18
The word of Yahweh is tried;
He is a shield unto all who take refuge in him.
For who is God, save Yahweh?
And who is a rock, besides our God,
The God that girds me with strength,
And makes my way perfect?
He makes my feet like the feet of a deer:
And sets me upon my high places.

REFRAIN
He spoke by the mouth of his holy prophets.

THE LORD'S PRAYER
Our Father in heaven
Hallowed be your name
Your kingdom come
Your will be done
On earth as it is in heaven
Give us this day our daily bread
Forgive us our debts as we forgive our debtors
Lead us not into temptation
But deliver us from the evil one
For yours is the kingdom and the power and the glory
Forever and ever

SHEMA & THE JESUS CREED
Hear, O Israel:
The Lord is our God, the Lord alone. You shall love the Lord your God with all your heart, and with all your soul and with all your might. You shall love your neighbor as yourself. There is no commandment greater than these.

CLOSING
We say yes! Amen!
Come Lord Jesus.

DAY 10
NOON
—

REFRAIN
He spoke by the mouth of his holy prophets.

† SILENCE

THE LORD'S PRAYER
Our Father in heaven
Hallowed be your name
Your kingdom come
Your will be done
On earth as it is in heaven
Give us this day our daily bread
Forgive us our debts as we forgive our debtors
Lead us not into temptation
But deliver us from the evil one
For yours is the kingdom and the power and the glory
Forever and ever

SHEMA & THE JESUS CREED
Hear, O Israel:
The Lord is our God, the Lord alone. You shall love the Lord your God with all your heart, and with all your soul and with all your might. You shall love your neighbor as yourself. There is no commandment greater than these.

CLOSING
We say yes! Amen!
Come Lord Jesus.

DAY 10
EVENING
—

REFRAIN
He spoke by the mouth of his holy prophets.

† SILENCE

THE BENEDICTUS
He spoke by the mouth of his holy prophets.

Blessed be the Lord,
The God of Israel,
For he has visited
And worked redemption for his people,
And has raised up a horn of salvation for us
In the house of his servant David
As he spoke by the mouth of his holy prophets
That have been from old,
Salvation from our enemies,
And from the hand of all that hate us;
To show mercy towards our fathers,
And to remember his holy covenant;
The oath which he swore to Abraham, our father,
To grant to us, that we being delivered
Out of the hand of our enemies
Should serve him without fear,
In holiness and righteousness
Before him all our days.

He spoke by the mouth of his holy prophets.

Yea and you, child,
Will be called the prophet of the Most High:
For you will go before the face of the Lord
To prepare his ways;
To give knowledge of salvation to his people
In the forgiveness of their sins,

He spoke by the mouth of his holy prophets.

Because of the tender mercy of our God,
Whereby the dayspring from on high will visit us,
To shine upon them that sit
In darkness and the shadow of death;
To guide our feet into the way of peace.

† SILENCE

REFRAIN
He spoke by the mouth of his holy prophets.

PSALM 33
For the word of Yahweh is right;
And all his work is done in faithfulness.
He loves righteousness and justice:
The earth is full of the lovingkindness of Yahweh.

REFRAIN
He spoke by the mouth of his holy prophets.

THE LORD'S PRAYER
Our Father in heaven
Hallowed be your name
Your kingdom come
Your will be done
On earth as it is in heaven
Give us this day our daily bread
Forgive us our debts as we forgive our debtors
Lead us not into temptation
But deliver us from the evil one
For yours is the kingdom and the power and the glory
Forever and ever

SHEMA & THE JESUS CREED
Hear, O Israel:
The Lord is our God, the Lord alone. You shall love the Lord your God with all your heart, and with all your soul and with all your might. You shall love your neighbor as yourself. There is no commandment greater than these.

CLOSING
We say yes! Amen!
Come Lord Jesus.

DAY 11
MORNING
—

REFRAIN
Shine upon them that sit in darkness.

† SILENCE

THE BENEDICTUS
Blessed be the Lord,
The God of Israel,
For he has visited
And worked redemption for his people,
And has raised up a horn of salvation for us
In the house of his servant David
As he spoke by the mouth of his holy prophets
That have been from old,
Salvation from our enemies,
And from the hand of all that hate us;
To show mercy towards our fathers,
And to remember his holy covenant;
The oath which he swore to Abraham, our father,
To grant to us, that we being delivered
Out of the hand of our enemies
Should serve him without fear,
In holiness and righteousness
Before him all our days.
Yea and you, child,
Will be called the prophet of the Most High:
For you will go before the face of the Lord
To prepare his ways;
To give knowledge of salvation to his people
In the forgiveness of their sins,
Because of the tender mercy of our God,
Whereby the dayspring from on high will visit us,
To shine upon them that sit
In darkness and the shadow of death;
To guide our feet into the way of peace.

† SILENCE

REFRAIN
Shine upon them that sit in darkness.

PSALM 67
God be merciful unto us, and bless us,
And cause his face to shine upon us;
Selah
That your way may be known upon the earth,
Your salvation among all nations.
Let the peoples praise you, O God;
Let all the peoples praise you.

REFRAIN
Shine upon them that sit in darkness.

THE LORD'S PRAYER
Our Father in heaven
Hallowed be your name
Your kingdom come
Your will be done
On earth as it is in heaven
Give us this day our daily bread
Forgive us our debts as we forgive our debtors
Lead us not into temptation
But deliver us from the evil one
For yours is the kingdom and the power and the glory
Forever and ever

SHEMA & THE JESUS CREED
Hear, O Israel:
The Lord is our God, the Lord alone. You shall love the Lord your God with all your heart, and with all your soul and with all your might. You shall love your neighbor as yourself. There is no commandment greater than these.

CLOSING
We say yes! Amen!
Come Lord Jesus.

DAY 11
NOON

—

REFRAIN
Shine upon them that sit in darkness.

† SILENCE

THE LORD'S PRAYER
Our Father in heaven
Hallowed be your name
Your kingdom come
Your will be done
On earth as it is in heaven
Give us this day our daily bread
Forgive us our debts as we forgive our debtors
Lead us not into temptation
But deliver us from the evil one
For yours is the kingdom and the power and the glory
Forever and ever

SHEMA & THE JESUS CREED
Hear, O Israel:
The Lord is our God, the Lord alone. You shall love the Lord your God with all your heart, and with all your soul and with all your might. You shall love your neighbor as yourself. There is no commandment greater than these.

CLOSING
We say yes! Amen!
Come Lord Jesus.

DAY 11
EVENING

—

REFRAIN
Shine upon them that sit in darkness.

† SILENCE

THE BENEDICTUS
Shine upon them that sit in darkness.

Blessed be the Lord,
The God of Israel,
For he has visited
And worked redemption for his people,
And has raised up a horn of salvation for us
In the house of his servant David

Shine upon them that sit in darkness.

As he spoke by the mouth of his holy prophets
That have been from old,
Salvation from our enemies,
And from the hand of all that hate us;
To show mercy towards our fathers,
And to remember his holy covenant;
The oath which he swore to Abraham, our father,
To grant to us, that we being delivered
Out of the hand of our enemies
Should serve him without fear,
In holiness and righteousness
Before him all our days.

Shine upon them that sit in darkness.

Yea and you, child,
Will be called the prophet of the Most High:
For you will go before the face of the Lord
To prepare his ways;
To give knowledge of salvation to his people
In the forgiveness of their sins,
Because of the tender mercy of our God,
Whereby the dayspring from on high will visit us,
To shine upon them that sit
In darkness and the shadow of death;
To guide our feet into the way of peace.

† SILENCE

REFRAIN
Shine upon them that sit in darkness.

PSALM 80
We will not turn away from you:
Quicken us, and we will call upon your name.
Turn us again, O Yahweh God of hosts;
Cause your face to shine, and we shall be saved.

REFRAIN
Shine upon them that sit in darkness.

THE LORD'S PRAYER
Our Father in heaven
Hallowed be your name
Your kingdom come
Your will be done
On earth as it is in heaven
Give us this day our daily bread
Forgive us our debts as we forgive our debtors
Lead us not into temptation
But deliver us from the evil one
For yours is the kingdom and the power and the glory
Forever and ever

SHEMA & THE JESUS CREED
Hear, O Israel:
The Lord is our God, the Lord alone. You shall love the Lord your God with all your heart, and with all your soul and with all your might. You shall love your neighbor as yourself. There is no commandment greater than these.

CLOSING
We say yes! Amen!
Come Lord Jesus.

DAY 12
MORNING
—

REFRAIN
Guide our feet.

† SILENCE

THE BENEDICTUS
Blessed be the Lord,
The God of Israel,
For he has visited
And worked redemption for his people,
And has raised up a horn of salvation for us
In the house of his servant David
As he spoke by the mouth of his holy prophets
That have been from old,
Salvation from our enemies,
And from the hand of all that hate us;
To show mercy towards our fathers,
And to remember his holy covenant;
The oath which he swore to Abraham, our father,
To grant to us, that we being delivered
Out of the hand of our enemies
Should serve him without fear,
In holiness and righteousness
Before him all our days.
Yea and you, child,
Will be called the prophet of the Most High:
For you will go before the face of the Lord
To prepare his ways;
To give knowledge of salvation to his people
In the forgiveness of their sins,
Because of the tender mercy of our God,
Whereby the dayspring from on high will visit us,
To shine upon them that sit
In darkness and the shadow of death;
To guide our feet into the way of peace.

† SILENCE

REFRAIN
Guide our feet.

PSALM 117
For you have delivered
My soul from death,
My eyes from tears,
And my feet from falling.
I will walk before Yahweh
In the land of the living.

REFRAIN
Guide our feet.

THE LORD'S PRAYER
Our Father in heaven
Hallowed be your name
Your kingdom come
Your will be done
On earth as it is in heaven
Give us this day our daily bread
Forgive us our debts as we forgive our debtors
Lead us not into temptation
But deliver us from the evil one
For yours is the kingdom and the power and the glory
Forever and ever

SHEMA & THE JESUS CREED
Hear, O Israel:
The Lord is our God, the Lord alone. You shall love the Lord your God with all your heart, and with all your soul and with all your might. You shall love your neighbor as yourself. There is no commandment greater than these.

CLOSING
We say yes! Amen!
Come Lord Jesus.

DAY 12
NOON
—

REFRAIN
Guide our feet.

† SILENCE

THE LORD'S PRAYER
Our Father in heaven
Hallowed be your name
Your kingdom come
Your will be done
On earth as it is in heaven
Give us this day our daily bread
Forgive us our debts as we forgive our debtors
Lead us not into temptation
But deliver us from the evil one
For yours is the kingdom and the power and the glory
Forever and ever

SHEMA & THE JESUS CREED
Hear, O Israel:
The Lord is our God, the Lord alone. You shall love the Lord your God with all your heart, and with all your soul and with all your might. You shall love your neighbor as yourself. There is no commandment greater than these.

CLOSING
We say yes! Amen!
Come Lord Jesus.

DAY 12
EVENING
—

REFRAIN
Guide our feet.

† SILENCE

A Prayer Guide for Advent

THE BENEDICTUS
Guide our feet.

Blessed be the Lord,
The God of Israel,
For he has visited
And worked redemption for his people,
And has raised up a horn of salvation for us
In the house of his servant David
As he spoke by the mouth of his holy prophets
That have been from old,

Guide our feet.

Salvation from our enemies,
And from the hand of all that hate us;
To show mercy towards our fathers,
And to remember his holy covenant;
The oath which he swore to Abraham, our father,
To grant to us, that we being delivered
Out of the hand of our enemies
Should serve him without fear,
In holiness and righteousness
Before him all our days.

Guide our feet.

Yea and you, child,
Will be called the prophet of the Most High:
For you will go before the face of the Lord
To prepare his ways;
To give knowledge of salvation to his people
In the forgiveness of their sins,
Because of the tender mercy of our God,
Whereby the dayspring from on high will visit us,
To shine upon them that sit
In darkness and the shadow of death;
To guide our feet into the way of peace.

† SILENCE

REFRAIN
Guide our feet.

PSALM 31
You have set my feet in a large place.
Have mercy upon me, O Yahweh,
For I am in distress:
My eyes waste away with grief,
Yes, my soul and my body.

REFRAIN
Guide our feet.

THE LORD'S PRAYER
Our Father in heaven
Hallowed be your name
Your kingdom come
Your will be done
On earth as it is in heaven
Give us this day our daily bread
Forgive us our debts as we forgive our debtors
Lead us not into temptation
But deliver us from the evil one
For yours is the kingdom and the power and the glory
Forever and ever

SHEMA & THE JESUS CREED
Hear, O Israel:
The Lord is our God, the Lord alone. You shall love the Lord
your God with all your heart, and with all your soul and with all
your might. You shall love your neighbor as yourself. There is no
commandment greater than these.

CLOSING
We say yes! Amen!
Come Lord Jesus.

DAY 13
MORNING
—

REFRAIN
Blessed be the Lord.

† SILENCE

THE BENEDICTUS
Blessed be the Lord,
The God of Israel,
For he has visited
And worked redemption for his people,
And has raised up a horn of salvation for us
In the house of his servant David
As he spoke by the mouth of his holy prophets
That have been from old,
Salvation from our enemies,
And from the hand of all that hate us;
To show mercy towards our fathers,
And to remember his holy covenant;
The oath which he swore to Abraham, our father,
To grant to us, that we being delivered
Out of the hand of our enemies
Should serve him without fear,
In holiness and righteousness
Before him all our days.
Yea and you, child,
Will be called the prophet of the Most High:
For you will go before the face of the Lord
To prepare his ways;
To give knowledge of salvation to his people
In the forgiveness of their sins,
Because of the tender mercy of our God,
Whereby the dayspring from on high will visit us,
To shine upon them that sit
In darkness and the shadow of death;
To guide our feet into the way of peace.

† SILENCE

REFRAIN
Blessed be the Lord.

PSALM 66
God has heard;
He has attended
To the voice of my prayer.
Blessed be God,
Who has not turned away my prayer,
Nor his lovingkindness from me.

REFRAIN
Blessed be the Lord.

THE LORD'S PRAYER
Our Father in heaven
Hallowed be your name
Your kingdom come
Your will be done
On earth as it is in heaven
Give us this day our daily bread
Forgive us our debts as we forgive our debtors
Lead us not into temptation
But deliver us from the evil one
For yours is the kingdom and the power and the glory
Forever and ever

SHEMA & THE JESUS CREED
Hear, O Israel:
The Lord is our God, the Lord alone. You shall love the Lord your God with all your heart, and with all your soul and with all your might. You shall love your neighbor as yourself. There is no commandment greater than these.

CLOSING
We say yes! Amen!
Come Lord Jesus.

DAY 13
NOON

—

REFRAIN
Blessed be the Lord.

† SILENCE

THE LORD'S PRAYER
Our Father in heaven
Hallowed be your name
Your kingdom come
Your will be done
On earth as it is in heaven
Give us this day our daily bread
Forgive us our debts as we forgive our debtors
Lead us not into temptation
But deliver us from the evil one
For yours is the kingdom and the power and the glory
Forever and ever

SHEMA & THE JESUS CREED
Hear, O Israel:
The Lord is our God, the Lord alone. You shall love the Lord your God with all your heart, and with all your soul and with all your might. You shall love your neighbor as yourself. There is no commandment greater than these.

CLOSING
We say yes! Amen!
Come Lord Jesus.

DAY 13
EVENING
—

REFRAIN
Blessed be the Lord.

† SILENCE

THE BENEDICTUS
Blessed be the Lord,
The God of Israel,
For he has visited
And worked redemption for his people,
And has raised up a horn of salvation for us
In the house of his servant David
As he spoke by the mouth of his holy prophets
That have been from old,

Blessed be the Lord.

Salvation from our enemies,
And from the hand of all that hate us;
To show mercy towards our fathers,
And to remember his holy covenant;
The oath which he swore to Abraham, our father,
To grant to us, that we being delivered
Out of the hand of our enemies
Should serve him without fear,
In holiness and righteousness
Before him all our days.

Blessed be the Lord.

Yea and you, child,
Will be called the prophet of the Most High:
For you will go before the face of the Lord
To prepare his ways;
To give knowledge of salvation to his people
In the forgiveness of their sins,
Because of the tender mercy of our God,

Whereby the dayspring from on high will visit us,
To shine upon them that sit
In darkness and the shadow of death;
To guide our feet into the way of peace.

Blessed be the Lord.

† SILENCE

REFRAIN
Blessed be the Lord.

PSALM 72
His name shall endure forever;
His name shall be continued as long as the sun:
And men shall be blessed in him;
All nations shall call him happy.
Blessed be Yahweh God, the God of Israel,
Who only does wondrous things:
And blessed be his glorious name forever;
And let the whole earth be filled with his glory.
Amen, and Amen.

REFRAIN
Blessed be the Lord.

THE LORD'S PRAYER
Our Father in heaven
Hallowed be your name
Your kingdom come
Your will be done
On earth as it is in heaven
Give us this day our daily bread
Forgive us our debts as we forgive our debtors
Lead us not into temptation
But deliver us from the evil one
For yours is the kingdom and the power and the glory
Forever and ever

SHEMA & THE JESUS CREED
Hear, O Israel:
The Lord is our God, the Lord alone. You shall love the Lord your God with all your heart, and with all your soul and with all your might. You shall love your neighbor as yourself. There is no commandment greater than these.

CLOSING
We say yes! Amen!
Come Lord Jesus.

DAY 14
MORNING
—

REFRAIN
Worked redemption for his people.

† SILENCE

THE BENEDICTUS
Blessed be the Lord,
The God of Israel,
For he has visited
And worked redemption for his people,
And has raised up a horn of salvation for us
In the house of his servant David
As he spoke by the mouth of his holy prophets
That have been from old,
Salvation from our enemies,
And from the hand of all that hate us;
To show mercy towards our fathers,
And to remember his holy covenant;
The oath which he swore to Abraham, our father,
To grant to us, that we being delivered
Out of the hand of our enemies
Should serve him without fear,
In holiness and righteousness
Before him all our days.
Yea and you, child,
Will be called the prophet of the Most High:
For you will go before the face of the Lord
To prepare his ways;
To give knowledge of salvation to his people
In the forgiveness of their sins,
Because of the tender mercy of our God,
Whereby the dayspring from on high will visit us,
To shine upon them that sit
In darkness and the shadow of death;
To guide our feet into the way of peace.

† SILENCE

REFRAIN
Worked redemption for his people.

PSALM 77
I will make mention of the deeds of Yahweh;
For I will remember your wonders of old.
I will meditate also upon all your work,
And muse on your doings.
Your way, O God, is in the sanctuary:
Who is a great god like God?
You are the God that does wonders:
You have made known your strength among the peoples.

REFRAIN
Worked redemption for his people.

THE LORD'S PRAYER
Our Father in heaven
Hallowed be your name
Your kingdom come
Your will be done
On earth as it is in heaven
Give us this day our daily bread
Forgive us our debts as we forgive our debtors
Lead us not into temptation
But deliver us from the evil one
For yours is the kingdom and the power and the glory
Forever and ever

SHEMA & THE JESUS CREED
Hear, O Israel:
The Lord is our God, the Lord alone. You shall love the Lord your God with all your heart, and with all your soul and with all your might. You shall love your neighbor as yourself. There is no commandment greater than these.

CLOSING
We say yes! Amen!
Come Lord Jesus.

DAY 14
NOON
—

REFRAIN
Worked redemption for his people.

† SILENCE

THE LORD'S PRAYER
Our Father in heaven
Hallowed be your name
Your kingdom come
Your will be done
On earth as it is in heaven
Give us this day our daily bread
Forgive us our debts as we forgive our debtors
Lead us not into temptation
But deliver us from the evil one
For yours is the kingdom and the power and the glory
Forever and ever

SHEMA & THE JESUS CREED
Hear, O Israel:
The Lord is our God, the Lord alone. You shall love the Lord your God with all your heart, and with all your soul and with all your might. You shall love your neighbor as yourself. There is no commandment greater than these.

CLOSING
We say yes! Amen!
Come Lord Jesus.

DAY 14
EVENING
—

REFRAIN
Worked redemption for his people.

† SILENCE

THE BENEDICTUS
Blessed be the Lord,
The God of Israel,
For he has visited
And worked redemption for his people,
And has raised up a horn of salvation for us
In the house of his servant David
As he spoke by the mouth of his holy prophets
That have been from old,
Salvation from our enemies,
And from the hand of all that hate us;
To show mercy towards our fathers,
And to remember his holy covenant;
The oath which he swore to Abraham, our father,

Worked redemption for his people.

To grant to us, that we being delivered
Out of the hand of our enemies
Should serve him without fear,
In holiness and righteousness
Before him all our days.

Worked redemption for his people.

Yea and you, child,
Will be called the prophet of the Most High:
For you will go before the face of the Lord
To prepare his ways;
To give knowledge of salvation to his people
In the forgiveness of their sins,

Worked redemption for his people.

Because of the tender mercy of our God,
Whereby the dayspring from on high will visit us,
To shine upon them that sit
In darkness and the shadow of death;
To guide our feet into the way of peace.

Worked redemption for his people.

† SILENCE

REFRAIN
Worked redemption for his people.

PSALM 92
For you, Yahweh, have made me glad through your work:
I will rejoice in the works of your hands.
How great are your works, O Yahweh!
Your thoughts are very deep.

REFRAIN
Worked redemption for his people.

THE LORD'S PRAYER
Our Father in heaven
Hallowed be your name
Your kingdom come
Your will be done
On earth as it is in heaven
Give us this day our daily bread
Forgive us our debts as we forgive our debtors
Lead us not into temptation
But deliver us from the evil one
For yours is the kingdom and the power and the glory
Forever and ever

SHEMA & THE JESUS CREED
Hear, O Israel:
The Lord is our God, the Lord alone. You shall love the Lord

your God with all your heart, and with all your soul and with all your might. You shall love your neighbor as yourself. There is no commandment greater than these.

CLOSING
We say yes! Amen!
Come Lord Jesus.

A PRAYER GUIDE FOR ADVENT
WEEK THREE

DAY 15
MORNING

—

REFRAIN
You prepared.

† SILENCE

THE NUNC DIMITTIS
Now let your servant depart, Lord
According to your word,
In peace
For my eyes have seen your salvation,
Which you prepared
Before the face of all peoples;
A light for revelation to the Gentiles,
And the glory of your people Israel.

† SILENCE

REFRAIN
You prepared.

PSALM 10
Yahweh is King forever and ever:
The nations will perish from his land.
Yahweh, you have heard the desire of the meek:
You will prepare their heart,
You will cause your ear to hear;
To judge the fatherless and the oppressed,
That man who is of the earth may be terrible no more.

REFRAIN
You prepared.

THE LORD'S PRAYER
Our Father in heaven,
Hallowed be your name.
Your kingdom come.
Your will be done,

On earth as it is in heaven.
Give us this day our daily bread.
Forgive us our debts, as we forgive our debtors.
Lead us not into temptation,
But deliver us from the evil one.
For yours is the kingdom and the power and the glory
Forever and ever.

SHEMA & THE JESUS CREED
Hear, O Israel:
The Lord is our God, the Lord alone. You shall love the Lord your God with all your heart, and with all your soul and with all your might. You shall love your neighbor as yourself. There is no commandment greater than these.

CLOSING
We say yes! Amen!
Come Lord Jesus.

DAY 15
NOON
—

REFRAIN
You prepared.

† SILENCE

THE LORD'S PRAYER
Our Father in heaven,
Hallowed be your name.
Your kingdom come.
Your will be done,
On earth as it is in heaven.
Give us this day our daily bread.
Forgive us our debts, as we forgive our debtors.
Lead us not into temptation,
But deliver us from the evil one.
For yours is the kingdom and the power and the glory
Forever and ever.

SHEMA & THE JESUS CREED
Hear, O Israel:
The Lord is our God, the Lord alone. You shall love the Lord your God with all your heart, and with all your soul and with all your might. You shall love your neighbor as yourself. There is no commandment greater than these.

CLOSING
We say yes! Amen!
Come Lord Jesus.

DAY 15
EVENING
—

REFRAIN
You prepared.

† SILENCE

THE NUNC DIMITTIS
You prepared.

Now let your servant depart, Lord
According to your word,
In peace

You prepared.

For my eyes have seen your salvation,
Which you prepared
Before the face of all peoples;
A light for revelation to the Gentiles,
And the glory of your people Israel.

† SILENCE

REFRAIN
You prepared.

PSALM 23
Yahweh is my shepherd; I shall not want.
He makes me to lie down in green pastures;
He leads me beside still waters.
He restores my soul:
He guides me in the paths of righteousness for his name's sake.
Yea, though I walk through the valley of the shadow of death,
I will fear no evil; for you are with me;
Your rod and your staff, they comfort me.
You prepare a table before me in the presence of my enemies:
You have anointed my head with oil;
My cup runs over.
Surely goodness and lovingkindness
Shall follow me all the days of my life;
And I shall dwell in the house of Yahweh forever.

REFRAIN
You prepared.

THE LORD'S PRAYER
Our Father in heaven,
Hallowed be your name.
Your kingdom come.
Your will be done,
On earth as it is in heaven.
Give us this day our daily bread.
Forgive us our debts, as we forgive our debtors.
Lead us not into temptation,
But deliver us from the evil one.
For yours is the kingdom and the power and the glory
Forever and ever.

SHEMA & THE JESUS CREED
Hear, O Israel:
The Lord is our God, the Lord alone. You shall love the Lord your God with all your heart, and with all your soul and with all your might. You shall love your neighbor as yourself. There is no commandment greater than these.

CLOSING
We say yes! Amen!
Come Lord Jesus.

DAY 16
MORNING
—

REFRAIN
Before the face of all peoples.

† SILENCE

THE NUNC DIMITTIS
Now let your servant depart, Lord
According to your word,
In peace
For my eyes have seen your salvation,
Which you prepared
Before the face of all peoples;
A light for revelation to the Gentiles,
And the glory of your people Israel.

† SILENCE

REFRAIN
Before the face of all peoples.

PSALM 22
And stand in awe of him,
All you the seed of Israel.
For he has not despised nor abhorred
The affliction of the afflicted;
Neither has he hid his face from them;
But when he cried unto him, he heard.

REFRAIN
Before the face of all peoples.

THE LORD'S PRAYER
Our Father in heaven,
Hallowed be your name.
Your kingdom come.
Your will be done,
On earth as it is in heaven.

Give us this day our daily bread.
Forgive us our debts, as we forgive our debtors.
Lead us not into temptation,
But deliver us from the evil one.
For yours is the kingdom and the power and the glory
Forever and ever.

SHEMA & THE JESUS CREED
Hear, O Israel:
The Lord is our God, the Lord alone. You shall love the Lord your God with all your heart, and with all your soul and with all your might. You shall love your neighbor as yourself. There is no commandment greater than these.

CLOSING
We say yes! Amen!
Come Lord Jesus.

DAY 16
NOON
—

REFRAIN
Before the face of all peoples.

† SILENCE

THE LORD'S PRAYER
Our Father in heaven,
Hallowed be your name.
Your kingdom come.
Your will be done,
On earth as it is in heaven.
Give us this day our daily bread.
Forgive us our debts, as we forgive our debtors.
Lead us not into temptation,
But deliver us from the evil one.
For yours is the kingdom and the power and the glory
Forever and ever.

A Prayer Guide for Advent

SHEMA & THE JESUS CREED
Hear, O Israel:
The Lord is our God, the Lord alone. You shall love the Lord your God with all your heart, and with all your soul and with all your might. You shall love your neighbor as yourself. There is no commandment greater than these.

CLOSING
We say yes! Amen!
Come Lord Jesus.

DAY 16
EVENING
—

REFRAIN
Before the face of all peoples.

† SILENCE

THE NUNC DIMITTIS
Before the face of all peoples.

Now let your servant depart, Lord
According to your word,
In peace
For my eyes have seen your salvation,
Which you prepared
Before the face of all peoples;
A light for revelation to the Gentiles,
And the glory of your people Israel.

Before the face of all peoples.

† SILENCE

REFRAIN
Before the face of all peoples.

PSALM 50
The Mighty One, God, Yahweh, has spoken,
And called the earth
From the rising of the sun
Unto the going down thereof.
Out of Zion, the perfection of beauty,
God shines forth.
Our God comes, and does not keep silence:
A fire devours before him,
And it is very tempestuous round about him.
He calls to the heavens above,
And to the earth, that he may judge his people:
Gather my saints together unto me,
Those that have made a covenant with me by sacrifice.
And the heavens shall declare his righteousness;
For God is judge himself.

REFRAIN
Before the face of all peoples.

THE LORD'S PRAYER
Our Father in heaven,
Hallowed be your name.
Your kingdom come.
Your will be done,
On earth as it is in heaven.
Give us this day our daily bread.
Forgive us our debts, as we forgive our debtors.
Lead us not into temptation,
But deliver us from the evil one.
For yours is the kingdom and the power and the glory
Forever and ever.

SHEMA & THE JESUS CREED
Hear, O Israel:
The Lord is our God, the Lord alone. You shall love the Lord your God with all your heart, and with all your soul and with all your might. You shall love your neighbor as yourself. There is no commandment greater than these.

CLOSING
We say yes! Amen!
Come Lord Jesus.

DAY 17
MORNING
—

REFRAIN
A light for revelation.

† SILENCE

THE NUNC DIMITTIS
Now let your servant depart, Lord
According to your word,
In peace
For my eyes have seen your salvation,
Which you prepared
Before the face of all peoples;
A light for revelation to the Gentiles,
And the glory of your people Israel.

† SILENCE

REFRAIN
A light for revelation.

PSALM 74
Yet God is my King of old,
Working salvation in the midst of the earth.
You did divide the sea by your strength:
You break the heads
Of the sea-monsters in the waters.
You break the heads
Of leviathan in pieces;
You gave him to be food to the people inhabiting the wilderness.
You did cleave fountain and flood:
You dried up mighty rivers.
The day is yours,
The night also is yours:
You have prepared the light and the sun.
You have set all the borders of the earth:
You have made summer and winter.

REFRAIN
A light for revelation.

THE LORD'S PRAYER
Our Father in heaven,
Hallowed be your name.
Your kingdom come.
Your will be done,
On earth as it is in heaven.
Give us this day our daily bread.
Forgive us our debts, as we forgive our debtors.
Lead us not into temptation,
But deliver us from the evil one.
For yours is the kingdom and the power and the glory
Forever and ever.

SHEMA & THE JESUS CREED
Hear, O Israel:
The Lord is our God, the Lord alone. You shall love the Lord your God with all your heart, and with all your soul and with all your might. You shall love your neighbor as yourself. There is no commandment greater than these.

CLOSING
We say yes! Amen!
Come Lord Jesus.

DAY 17
NOON
—

REFRAIN
A light for revelation.

† **SILENCE**

THE LORD'S PRAYER
Our Father in heaven,
Hallowed be your name.

Your kingdom come.
Your will be done,
On earth as it is in heaven.
Give us this day our daily bread.
Forgive us our debts, as we forgive our debtors.
Lead us not into temptation,
But deliver us from the evil one.
For yours is the kingdom and the power and the glory
Forever and ever.

SHEMA & THE JESUS CREED
Hear, O Israel:
The Lord is our God, the Lord alone. You shall love the Lord your God with all your heart, and with all your soul and with all your might. You shall love your neighbor as yourself. There is no commandment greater than these.

CLOSING
We say yes! Amen!
Come Lord Jesus.

DAY 17
EVENING
—

REFRAIN
A light for revelation.

† SILENCE

THE NUNC DIMITTIS
A light for revelation.

Now let your servant depart, Lord
According to your word,
In peace
For my eyes have seen your salvation,
Which you prepared
Before the face of all peoples;

A light for revelation to the Gentiles,
And the glory of your people Israel.

A light for revelation.

† SILENCE

REFRAIN
A light for revelation.

PSALM 97
For you, Yahweh,
Are most high above all the earth:
You are exalted far above all gods.
O you that love Yahweh, hate evil:
He preserves the souls of his saints;
He delivers them out of the hand of the wicked.
Light is sown for the righteous,
And gladness for the upright in heart.

REFRAIN
A light for revelation.

THE LORD'S PRAYER
Our Father in heaven,
Hallowed be your name.
Your kingdom come.
Your will be done,
On earth as it is in heaven.
Give us this day our daily bread.
Forgive us our debts, as we forgive our debtors.
Lead us not into temptation,
But deliver us from the evil one.
For yours is the kingdom and the power and the glory
Forever and ever.

SHEMA & THE JESUS CREED
Hear, O Israel:
The Lord is our God, the Lord alone. You shall love the Lord
your God with all your heart, and with all your soul and with all

your might. You shall love your neighbor as yourself. There is no commandment greater than these.

CLOSING
We say yes! Amen!
Come Lord Jesus.

DAY 18
MORNING
—

REFRAIN
The glory of your people.

† SILENCE

THE NUNC DIMITTIS
Now let your servant depart, Lord
According to your word,
In peace
For my eyes have seen your salvation,
Which you prepared
Before the face of all peoples;
A light for revelation to the Gentiles,
And the glory of your people Israel.

† SILENCE

REFRAIN
The glory of your people.

PSALM 145
They will gush
Remembering your great goodness,
And will sing of your righteousness.
Yahweh is gracious, and merciful;
Slow to anger, and of great lovingkindness.
Yahweh is good to all;
And his tender mercies are over all his works.
All your work
Will give thanks to you, O Yahweh;
And your saints will bless you.
They will speak of the glory of your kingdom,
And talk of your power;
To make known to the sons of Adam his mighty acts,
And the glory of the majesty of his kingdom.
Your kingdom is an everlasting kingdom,
And your dominion endures throughout all generations.

Yahweh upholds all that fall,
And raises up all who are bowed down.
The eyes of all look to you;
And you give them their food in due season.

REFRAIN
The glory of your people.

THE LORD'S PRAYER
Our Father in heaven,
Hallowed be your name.
Your kingdom come.
Your will be done,
On earth as it is in heaven.
Give us this day our daily bread.
Forgive us our debts, as we forgive our debtors.
Lead us not into temptation,
But deliver us from the evil one.
For yours is the kingdom and the power and the glory
Forever and ever.

SHEMA & THE JESUS CREED
Hear, O Israel:
The Lord is our God, the Lord alone. You shall love the Lord your God with all your heart, and with all your soul and with all your might. You shall love your neighbor as yourself. There is no commandment greater than these.

CLOSING
We say yes! Amen!
Come Lord Jesus.

DAY 18
NOON

—

REFRAIN
The glory of your people.

† SILENCE

THE LORD'S PRAYER
Our Father in heaven,
Hallowed be your name.
Your kingdom come.
Your will be done,
On earth as it is in heaven.
Give us this day our daily bread.
Forgive us our debts, as we forgive our debtors.
Lead us not into temptation,
But deliver us from the evil one.
For yours is the kingdom and the power and the glory
Forever and ever.

SHEMA & THE JESUS CREED
Hear, O Israel:
The Lord is our God, the Lord alone. You shall love the Lord your God with all your heart, and with all your soul and with all your might. You shall love your neighbor as yourself. There is no commandment greater than these.

CLOSING
We say yes! Amen!
Come Lord Jesus.

DAY 18
EVENING

—

REFRAIN
The glory of your people.

† SILENCE

THE NUNC DIMITTIS
The glory of your people.

Now let your servant depart, Lord
According to your word,
In peace
For my eyes have seen your salvation,
Which you prepared
Before the face of all peoples;
A light for revelation to the Gentiles,
And the glory of your people Israel.

The glory of your people.

† SILENCE

REFRAIN
The glory of your people.

PSALM 79
Let your tender mercies speedily meet us;
For we are brought very low.
Help us, O God of our salvation, for the glory of your name;
And deliver us, and forgive our sins, for your name's sake.

REFRAIN
The glory of your people.

THE LORD'S PRAYER
Our Father in heaven,
Hallowed be your name.
Your kingdom come.
Your will be done,
On earth as it is in heaven.
Give us this day our daily bread.
Forgive us our debts, as we forgive our debtors.
Lead us not into temptation,
But deliver us from the evil one.
For yours is the kingdom and the power and the glory
Forever and ever.

SHEMA & THE JESUS CREED
Hear, O Israel:
The Lord is our God, the Lord alone. You shall love the Lord your God with all your heart, and with all your soul and with all your might. You shall love your neighbor as yourself. There is no commandment greater than these.

CLOSING
We say yes! Amen!
Come Lord Jesus.

DAY 19
MORNING
—

REFRAIN
My eyes have seen your salvation.

† SILENCE

THE NUNC DIMITTIS
Now let your servant depart, Lord
According to your word,
In peace
For my eyes have seen your salvation,
Which you prepared
Before the face of all peoples;
A light for revelation to the Gentiles,
And the glory of your people Israel.

† SILENCE

REFRAIN
My eyes have seen your salvation.

PSALM 118
I will give thanks unto you;
For you have answered me,
And have become my salvation.
The stone which the builders rejected
Has become the head of the corner.
This is Yahweh's doing;
It is marvelous in our eyes.
This is the day which Yahweh has made;
We will rejoice and be glad in it.

REFRAIN
My eyes have seen your salvation.

THE LORD'S PRAYER
Our Father in heaven,
Hallowed be your name.

Your kingdom come.
Your will be done,
On earth as it is in heaven.
Give us this day our daily bread.
Forgive us our debts, as we forgive our debtors.
Lead us not into temptation,
But deliver us from the evil one.
For yours is the kingdom and the power and the glory
Forever and ever.

SHEMA & THE JESUS CREED
Hear, O Israel:
The Lord is our God, the Lord alone. You shall love the Lord your God with all your heart, and with all your soul and with all your might. You shall love your neighbor as yourself. There is no commandment greater than these.

CLOSING
We say yes! Amen!
Come Lord Jesus.

DAY 19
NOON

—

REFRAIN
My eyes have seen your salvation.

† SILENCE

THE LORD'S PRAYER
Our Father in heaven,
Hallowed be your name.
Your kingdom come.
Your will be done,
On earth as it is in heaven.
Give us this day our daily bread.
Forgive us our debts, as we forgive our debtors.
Lead us not into temptation,

But deliver us from the evil one.
For yours is the kingdom and the power and the glory
Forever and ever.

SHEMA & THE JESUS CREED
Hear, O Israel:
The Lord is our God, the Lord alone. You shall love the Lord your God with all your heart, and with all your soul and with all your might. You shall love your neighbor as yourself. There is no commandment greater than these.

CLOSING
We say yes! Amen!
Come Lord Jesus.

DAY 19
EVENING

—

REFRAIN
My eyes have seen your salvation.

† SILENCE

THE NUNC DIMITTIS
My eyes have seen your salvation.

Now let your servant depart, Lord
According to your word,
In peace
For my eyes have seen your salvation,
Which you prepared
Before the face of all peoples;
A light for revelation to the Gentiles,
And the glory of your people Israel.

My eyes have seen your salvation.

† SILENCE

A Prayer Guide for Advent | 103

REFRAIN
My eyes have seen your salvation.

PSALM 131
Yahweh, my heart is not haughty,
Nor my eyes lofty;
Neither do I go after great matters,
Or things too wonderful for me.
Surely I have stilled and quieted my soul;
Like a weaned child with his mother,
Like a weaned child is my soul within me.
O Israel, hope in Yahweh
From this time forth
And forevermore.

THE LORD'S PRAYER
Our Father in heaven,
Hallowed be your name.
Your kingdom come.
Your will be done,
On earth as it is in heaven.
Give us this day our daily bread.
Forgive us our debts, as we forgive our debtors.
Lead us not into temptation,
But deliver us from the evil one.
For yours is the kingdom and the power and the glory
Forever and ever.

SHEMA & THE JESUS CREED
Hear, O Israel:
The Lord is our God, the Lord alone. You shall love the Lord your God with all your heart, and with all your soul and with all your might. You shall love your neighbor as yourself. There is no commandment greater than these.

CLOSING
We say yes! Amen!
Come Lord Jesus.

DAY 20
MORNING
—

REFRAIN
Let your servant depart, Lord.

† SILENCE

THE NUNC DIMITTIS
Now let your servant depart, Lord
According to your word,
In peace
For my eyes have seen your salvation,
Which you prepared
Before the face of all peoples;
A light for revelation to the Gentiles,
And the glory of your people Israel.

† SILENCE

REFRAIN
Let your servant depart, Lord.

PSALM 86
Bow down your ear,
O Yahweh answer me;
For I am poor and needy.
Preserve my soul; for I am godly:
O you my God,
Save your servant that trusts in you.
Be merciful unto me, O Lord;
For unto you do I cry all the day long.
Bring joy to the soul of your servant;
For unto you, O Lord, do I lift up my soul.
For you, Lord, are good, and ready to forgive,
And abundant in lovingkindness
Unto all who call upon you.
Give ear, O Yahweh, unto my prayer;
And hearken unto the voice of my supplications.

REFRAIN
Let your servant depart, Lord.

THE LORD'S PRAYER
Our Father in heaven,
Hallowed be your name.
Your kingdom come.
Your will be done,
On earth as it is in heaven.
Give us this day our daily bread.
Forgive us our debts, as we forgive our debtors.
Lead us not into temptation,
But deliver us from the evil one.
For yours is the kingdom and the power and the glory
Forever and ever.

SHEMA & THE JESUS CREED
Hear, O Israel:
The Lord is our God, the Lord alone. You shall love the Lord your God with all your heart, and with all your soul and with all your might. You shall love your neighbor as yourself. There is no commandment greater than these.

CLOSING
We say yes! Amen!
Come Lord Jesus.

DAY 20
NOON
—

REFRAIN
Let your servant depart, Lord.

† SILENCE

THE LORD'S PRAYER
Our Father in heaven,
Hallowed be your name.

Your kingdom come.
Your will be done,
On earth as it is in heaven.
Give us this day our daily bread.
Forgive us our debts, as we forgive our debtors.
Lead us not into temptation,
But deliver us from the evil one.
For yours is the kingdom and the power and the glory
Forever and ever.

SHEMA & THE JESUS CREED
Hear, O Israel:
The Lord is our God, the Lord alone. You shall love the Lord your God with all your heart, and with all your soul and with all your might. You shall love your neighbor as yourself. There is no commandment greater than these.

CLOSING
We say yes! Amen!
Come Lord Jesus.

DAY 20
EVENING
—

REFRAIN
Let your servant depart, Lord.

† SILENCE

THE NUNC DIMITTIS
Let your servant depart, Lord.

Now let your servant depart, Lord
According to your word,
In peace
For my eyes have seen your salvation,
Which you prepared
Before the face of all peoples;

A light for revelation to the Gentiles,
And the glory of your people Israel.

Let your servant depart, Lord.

† SILENCE

REFRAIN
Let your servant depart, Lord.

PSALM 117
Praise Yahweh, all you nations;
Laud him, all peoples.
For his lovingkindness
Is great toward us;
And the truth of Yahweh
Endures forever.
Praise Yahweh.

REFRAIN
Let your servant depart, Lord.

THE LORD'S PRAYER
Our Father in heaven,
Hallowed be your name.
Your kingdom come.
Your will be done,
On earth as it is in heaven.
Give us this day our daily bread.
Forgive us our debts, as we forgive our debtors.
Lead us not into temptation,
But deliver us from the evil one.
For yours is the kingdom and the power and the glory
Forever and ever.

SHEMA & THE JESUS CREED
Hear, O Israel:
The Lord is our God, the Lord alone. You shall love the Lord your God with all your heart, and with all your soul and with all your might. You shall love your neighbor as yourself. There is no commandment greater than these.

CLOSING
We say yes! Amen!
Come Lord Jesus.

DAY 21
MORNING
—

REFRAIN
According to your word.

† SILENCE

THE NUNC DIMITTIS
Now let your servant depart, Lord
According to your word,
In peace
For my eyes have seen your salvation,
Which you prepared
Before the face of all peoples;
A light for revelation to the Gentiles,
And the glory of your people Israel.

† SILENCE

REFRAIN
According to your word.

PSALM 109
Help me, O Yahweh my God,
Save me
According to your lovingkindness:
That they may know that this is your hand;
That you, Yahweh, have done it.
Let them curse,
But you bless:
When they arise, they shall be put to shame,
But your servant shall rejoice.

REFRAIN
According to your word.

THE LORD'S PRAYER
Our Father in heaven,
Hallowed be your name.

Your kingdom come.
Your will be done,
On earth as it is in heaven.
Give us this day our daily bread.
Forgive us our debts, as we forgive our debtors.
Lead us not into temptation,
But deliver us from the evil one.
For yours is the kingdom and the power and the glory
Forever and ever.

SHEMA & THE JESUS CREED
Hear, O Israel:
The Lord is our God, the Lord alone. You shall love the Lord your God with all your heart, and with all your soul and with all your might. You shall love your neighbor as yourself. There is no commandment greater than these.

CLOSING
We say yes! Amen!
Come Lord Jesus.

DAY 21
NOON
—

REFRAIN
According to your word.

† SILENCE

THE LORD'S PRAYER
Our Father in heaven,
Hallowed be your name.
Your kingdom come.
Your will be done,
On earth as it is in heaven.
Give us this day our daily bread.
Forgive us our debts, as we forgive our debtors.
Lead us not into temptation,
But deliver us from the evil one.

For yours is the kingdom and the power and the glory
Forever and ever.

SHEMA & THE JESUS CREED
Hear, O Israel:
The Lord is our God, the Lord alone. You shall love the Lord your God with all your heart, and with all your soul and with all your might. You shall love your neighbor as yourself. There is no commandment greater than these.

CLOSING
We say yes! Amen!
Come Lord Jesus.

DAY 21
EVENING
—

REFRAIN
According to your word.

† SILENCE

THE NUNC DIMITTIS
According to your word.

Now let your servant depart, Lord
According to your word,
In peace
For my eyes have seen your salvation,
Which you prepared
Before the face of all peoples;
A light for revelation to the Gentiles,
And the glory of your people Israel.

According to your word.

† SILENCE

REFRAIN
According to your word.

PSALM 119

Seven times a day do I praise you,
Because of your righteous ordinances.
Those who love your law have great peace.
And they have no occasion of stumbling.
I have hoped for your salvation, O Yahweh,
And have done your commandments.
My soul has observed your testimonies;
And I love them exceedingly.
I have observed your precepts and your testimonies;
For all my ways are before you.

REFRAIN
According to your word.

THE LORD'S PRAYER
Our Father in heaven,
Hallowed be your name.
Your kingdom come.
Your will be done,
On earth as it is in heaven.
Give us this day our daily bread.
Forgive us our debts, as we forgive our debtors.
Lead us not into temptation,
But deliver us from the evil one.
For yours is the kingdom and the power and the glory
Forever and ever.

SHEMA & THE JESUS CREED
Hear, O Israel:
The Lord is our God, the Lord alone. You shall love the Lord your God with all your heart, and with all your soul and with all your might. You shall love your neighbor as yourself. There is no commandment greater than these.

CLOSING
We say yes! Amen!
Come Lord Jesus.

A PRAYER GUIDE FOR ADVENT
WEEK FOUR

DAY 22
MORNING
—

REFRAIN
Behold, good tidings.

† SILENCE

GLORIA
The shining glory of the Lord
All around.
Do not be afraid.
Behold!
Good tidings of great joy
To all the people.
There is born to us
In the city of David
A Savior, who is Christ the Lord.
Glory to God in the highest heavens,
And on earth peace
Among men in whom he is well pleased.

† SILENCE

REFRAIN
Behold, good tidings.

PSALM 136
Oh give thanks unto Yahweh;
For he is good;
For his lovingkindness endures forever.
Oh give thanks unto the God of gods;
For his lovingkindness endures forever.
Oh give thanks unto the Lord of lords;
For his lovingkindness endures forever.
To him who alone does great wonders;
For his lovingkindness endures forever.

REFRAIN
Behold, good tidings.

THE LORD'S PRAYER
Our Father in heaven,
Hallowed be your name.
Your kingdom come.
Your will be done,
On earth as it is in heaven.
Give us this day our daily bread.
Forgive us our debts, as we forgive our debtors.
Lead us not into temptation,
But deliver us from the evil one.
For yours is the kingdom and the power and the glory
Forever and ever.

SHEMA & THE JESUS CREED
Hear, O Israel:
The Lord is our God, the Lord alone. You shall love the Lord your God with all your heart, and with all your soul and with all your might. You shall love your neighbor as yourself. There is no commandment greater than these.

CLOSING
We say yes! Amen!
Come Lord Jesus.

DAY 22
NOON
—

REFRAIN
Behold, good tidings.

† SILENCE

THE LORD'S PRAYER
Our Father in heaven,
Hallowed be your name.
Your kingdom come.
Your will be done,
On earth as it is in heaven.
Give us this day our daily bread.

Forgive us our debts, as we forgive our debtors.
Lead us not into temptation,
But deliver us from the evil one.
For yours is the kingdom and the power and the glory
Forever and ever.

SHEMA & THE JESUS CREED
Hear, O Israel:
The Lord is our God, the Lord alone. You shall love the Lord your God with all your heart, and with all your soul and with all your might. You shall love your neighbor as yourself. There is no commandment greater than these.

CLOSING
We say yes! Amen!
Come Lord Jesus.

DAY 22
EVENING
—

REFRAIN
Behold, good tidings.

† SILENCE

GLORIA
Behold, good tidings.

The shining glory of the Lord
All around.
Do not be afraid.
Behold,
Good tidings of great joy
To all the people.
There is born to us
In the city of David
A Savior, who is Christ the Lord.

Behold, good tidings.

A Prayer Guide for Advent

Glory to God in the highest heavens,
And on earth peace
Among men in whom he is well pleased.

Behold, good tidings.

† SILENCE

REFRAIN
Behold, good tidings.

PSALM 112
Blessed is the one that fears Yahweh,
That delights greatly in his commandments.
For he shall never be moved;
The righteous shall be forever remembered.
He shall not be afraid of evil tidings:
His heart is fixed,
Trusting in Yahweh.
His heart is established,
He shall not be afraid.

REFRAIN
Behold, good tidings.

THE LORD'S PRAYER
Our Father in heaven,
Hallowed be your name.
Your kingdom come.
Your will be done,
On earth as it is in heaven.
Give us this day our daily bread.
Forgive us our debts, as we forgive our debtors.
Lead us not into temptation,
But deliver us from the evil one.
For yours is the kingdom and the power and the glory
Forever and ever.

SHEMA & THE JESUS CREED
Hear, O Israel:
The Lord is our God, the Lord alone. You shall love the Lord your God with all your heart, and with all your soul and with all your might. You shall love your neighbor as yourself. There is no commandment greater than these.

CLOSING
We say yes! Amen!
Come Lord Jesus.

DAY 23
MORNING
—

REFRAIN
The shining glory of the Lord
All around.

† SILENCE

GLORIA
The shining glory of the Lord
All around.
Do not be afraid.
Behold,
Good tidings of great joy
To all the people.
There is born to us
In the city of David
A Savior, who is Christ the Lord.
Glory to God in the highest heavens,
And on earth peace
Among men in whom he is well pleased.

† SILENCE

REFRAIN
The shining glory of the Lord
All around.

PSALM 84
Behold, O God our shield,
And look upon the face of your anointed.
For a day in your courts
Is better than a thousand elsewhere.
I would rather be a doorkeeper
In the house of my God,
Than to dwell in the tents of wickedness.
For Yahweh God is a sun and a shield:
Yahweh will give grace and glory;
No good thing will he withhold

From those who walk uprightly.
O Yahweh of hosts,
Blessed is the one that trusts in you.

REFRAIN
The shining glory of the Lord
All around.

THE LORD'S PRAYER
Our Father in heaven,
Hallowed be your name.
Your kingdom come.
Your will be done,
On earth as it is in heaven.
Give us this day our daily bread.
Forgive us our debts, as we forgive our debtors.
Lead us not into temptation,
But deliver us from the evil one.
For yours is the kingdom and the power and the glory
Forever and ever.

SHEMA & THE JESUS CREED
Hear, O Israel:
The Lord is our God, the Lord alone. You shall love the Lord your God with all your heart, and with all your soul and with all your might. You shall love your neighbor as yourself. There is no commandment greater than these.

CLOSING
We say yes! Amen!
Come Lord Jesus.

DAY 23
NOON
—

REFRAIN
The shining glory of the Lord
All around.

† SILENCE

THE LORD'S PRAYER
Our Father in heaven,
Hallowed be your name.
Your kingdom come.
Your will be done,
On earth as it is in heaven.
Give us this day our daily bread.
Forgive us our debts, as we forgive our debtors.
Lead us not into temptation,
But deliver us from the evil one.
For yours is the kingdom and the power and the glory
Forever and ever.

SHEMA & THE JESUS CREED
Hear, O Israel:
The Lord is our God, the Lord alone. You shall love the Lord your God with all your heart, and with all your soul and with all your might. You shall love your neighbor as yourself. There is no commandment greater than these.

CLOSING
We say yes! Amen!
Come Lord Jesus.

DAY 23
EVENING

—

REFRAIN
The shining glory of the Lord
All around.

† SILENCE

GLORIA
The shining glory of the Lord
All around.
Do not be afraid.

Behold,
Good tidings of great joy
To all the people.
There is born to us
In the city of David
A Savior, who is Christ the Lord.

The shining glory of the Lord
All around.

Glory to God in the highest heavens,
And on earth peace
Among men in whom he is well pleased.

The shining glory of the Lord
All around.

† SILENCE

REFRAIN
The shining glory of the Lord
All around.

PSALM 80
Give ear, O Shepherd of Israel,
You that lead Joseph like a flock;
You that sit
Above the cherubim, shine forth.
Before Ephraim and Benjamin and Manasseh,
Stir up your might,
And come to save us.
Turn us again, O God;
And cause your face to shine,
And we shall be saved.

REFRAIN
The shining glory of the Lord
All around.

THE LORD'S PRAYER

Our Father in heaven,
Hallowed be your name.
Your kingdom come.
Your will be done,
On earth as it is in heaven.
Give us this day our daily bread.
Forgive us our debts, as we forgive our debtors.
Lead us not into temptation,
But deliver us from the evil one.
For yours is the kingdom and the power and the glory
Forever and ever.

SHEMA & THE JESUS CREED

Hear, O Israel:
The Lord is our God, the Lord alone. You shall love the Lord your God with all your heart, and with all your soul and with all your might. You shall love your neighbor as yourself. There is no commandment greater than these.

CLOSING

We say yes! Amen!
Come Lord Jesus.

DAY 24
MORNING
—

REFRAIN
Do not be afraid.

† SILENCE

GLORIA
The shining glory of the Lord
All around.
Do not be afraid.
Behold,
Good tidings of great joy
To all the people.
There is born to us
In the city of David
A Savior, who is Christ the Lord.
Glory to God in the highest heavens,
And on earth peace
Among men in whom he is well pleased.

† SILENCE

REFRAIN
Do not be afraid.

PSALM 91
He that dwells in the secret place
Of the Most High
Shall abide under the shadow
Of the Almighty.
I will say of Yahweh,
He is my refuge and my fortress;
My God, in whom I trust.
For he will deliver you
From the snare of the fowler,
And from the deadly pestilence.
He will cover you with his pinions,
And under his wings

You shall take refuge:
His truth is a shield and a buckler.
You shall not be afraid
Of the terror by night,
Nor of the arrow
That flies by day;
Nor of the pestilence
That walks in darkness,
Nor for the destruction
That wastes at noonday.

REFRAIN
Do not be afraid.

THE LORD'S PRAYER
Our Father in heaven,
Hallowed be your name.
Your kingdom come.
Your will be done,
On earth as it is in heaven.
Give us this day our daily bread.
Forgive us our debts, as we forgive our debtors.
Lead us not into temptation,
But deliver us from the evil one.
For yours is the kingdom and the power and the glory
Forever and ever.

SHEMA & THE JESUS CREED
Hear, O Israel:
The Lord is our God, the Lord alone. You shall love the Lord your God with all your heart, and with all your soul and with all your might. You shall love your neighbor as yourself. There is no commandment greater than these.

CLOSING
We say yes! Amen!
Come Lord Jesus.

DAY 24
NOON
—

REFRAIN
Do not be afraid.

† SILENCE

THE LORD'S PRAYER
Our Father in heaven,
Hallowed be your name.
Your kingdom come.
Your will be done,
On earth as it is in heaven.
Give us this day our daily bread.
Forgive us our debts, as we forgive our debtors.
Lead us not into temptation,
But deliver us from the evil one.
For yours is the kingdom and the power and the glory
Forever and ever.

SHEMA & THE JESUS CREED
Hear, O Israel:
The Lord is our God, the Lord alone. You shall love the Lord your God with all your heart, and with all your soul and with all your might. You shall love your neighbor as yourself. There is no commandment greater than these.

CLOSING
We say yes! Amen!
Come Lord Jesus.

DAY 24
EVENING
—

REFRAIN
Do not be afraid.

† SILENCE

GLORIA
Do not be afraid.

The shining glory of the Lord
All around.
Do not be afraid.
Behold,
Good tidings of great joy
To all the people.
There is born to us
In the city of David
A Savior, who is Christ the Lord.

Do not be afraid.

REFRAIN
Do not be afraid.

† SILENCE

REFRAIN
Do not be afraid.

PSALM 27
Yahweh is my light and my salvation;
Whom shall I fear?
Yahweh is the strength of my life;
Of whom shall I be afraid?
When evil-doers came upon me to eat my flesh,
Even mine adversaries and my foes, They stumbled and fell.
Though a host should encamp against me,
My heart shall not fear:

Though war should rise against me,
Even then will I be confident.
One thing have I asked of Yahweh, That I will seek after;
That I may dwell in the house of Yahweh
All the days of my life,
To behold the beauty of Yahweh,
And to seek in his temple.

REFRAIN
Do not be afraid.

THE LORD'S PRAYER
Our Father in heaven,
Hallowed be your name.
Your kingdom come.
Your will be done,
On earth as it is in heaven.
Give us this day our daily bread.
Forgive us our debts, as we forgive our debtors.
Lead us not into temptation,
But deliver us from the evil one.
For yours is the kingdom and the power and the glory
Forever and ever.

SHEMA & THE JESUS CREED
Hear, O Israel:
The Lord is our God, the Lord alone. You shall love the Lord your God with all your heart, and with all your soul and with all your might. You shall love your neighbor as yourself. There is no commandment greater than these.

CLOSING
We say yes! Amen!
Come Lord Jesus.

DAY 25
MORNING
—

REFRAIN
To all the people.

† SILENCE

GLORIA
The shining glory of the Lord
All around.
Do not be afraid.
Behold,
Good tidings of great joy
To all the people.
There is born to us
In the city of David
A Savior, who is Christ the Lord.
Glory to God in the highest heavens,
And on earth peace
Among men in whom he is well pleased.

† SILENCE

REFRAIN
To all the people.

PSALM 94
Unless Yahweh had been my help,
My soul had soon dwelt in silence.
When I said, My foot slips;
Your lovingkindness, O Yahweh,
Held me up.
In the multitude of my thoughts within me
Your comforts delight my soul.

REFRAIN
To all the people.

THE LORD'S PRAYER
Our Father in heaven,
Hallowed be your name.
Your kingdom come.
Your will be done,
On earth as it is in heaven.
Give us this day our daily bread.
Forgive us our debts, as we forgive our debtors.
Lead us not into temptation,
But deliver us from the evil one.
For yours is the kingdom and the power and the glory
Forever and ever.

SHEMA & THE JESUS CREED
Hear, O Israel:
The Lord is our God, the Lord alone. You shall love the Lord your God with all your heart, and with all your soul and with all your might. You shall love your neighbor as yourself. There is no commandment greater than these.

CLOSING
We say yes! Amen!
Come Lord Jesus.

DAY 25
NOON
—

REFRAIN
To all the people.

† SILENCE

THE LORD'S PRAYER
Our Father in heaven,
Hallowed be your name.
Your kingdom come.
Your will be done,
On earth as it is in heaven.
Give us this day our daily bread.

Forgive us our debts, as we forgive our debtors.
Lead us not into temptation,
But deliver us from the evil one.
For yours is the kingdom and the power and the glory
Forever and ever.

SHEMA & THE JESUS CREED
Hear, O Israel:
The Lord is our God, the Lord alone. You shall love the Lord your God with all your heart, and with all your soul and with all your might. You shall love your neighbor as yourself. There is no commandment greater than these.

CLOSING
We say yes! Amen!
Come Lord Jesus.

DAY 25
EVENING

REFRAIN
To all the people.

| SILENCE

GLORIA
To all the people.

The shining glory of the Lord
All around.
Do not be afraid.
Behold,
Good tidings of great joy
To all the people.
There is born to us
In the city of David
A Savior, who is Christ the Lord.

To all the people.

Glory to God in the highest heavens,
And on earth peace
Among men in whom he is well pleased.

† SILENCE

REFRAIN
To all the people.

PSALM 47
Oh clap your hands,
All you peoples;
Shout unto God
With the voice of triumph.
For Yahweh Most High is awesome
He is a great King
Over all the earth.
For God is the King of all the earth:
Sing praises with understanding.
God reigns over the nations:
God sits upon his holy throne.
The princes of the peoples
Are gathered together
To be the people of the God of Abraham:
For the shields of the earth
Belong unto God;
He is greatly exalted.

REFRAIN
To all the people.

THE LORD'S PRAYER
Our Father in heaven,
Hallowed be your name.
Your kingdom come.
Your will be done,
On earth as it is in heaven.
Give us this day our daily bread.
Forgive us our debts, as we forgive our debtors.
Lead us not into temptation,

But deliver us from the evil one.
For yours is the kingdom and the power and the glory
Forever and ever.

SHEMA & THE JESUS CREED
Hear, O Israel:
The Lord is our God, the Lord alone. You shall love the Lord your God with all your heart, and with all your soul and with all your might. You shall love your neighbor as yourself. There is no commandment greater than these.

CLOSING
We say yes! Amen!
Come Lord Jesus.

DAY 26
MORNING
—

REFRAIN
Peace among men in whom he is well pleased.

† SILENCE

GLORIA
The shining glory of the Lord
All around.
Do not be afraid.
Behold,
Good tidings of great joy
To all the people.
There is born to us
In the city of David
A Savior, who is Christ the Lord.
Glory to God in the highest heavens,
And on earth peace
Among men in whom he is well pleased.

† SILENCE

REFRAIN
Peace among men in whom he is well pleased.

PSALM 108
I will give thanks unto you,
O Yahweh, among the peoples;
And I will sing praises unto you among the nations.
For your lovingkindness is great above the heavens;
And your truth reaches unto the skies.
Be exalted, O God,
Above the heavens,
And your glory above all the earth.
That your beloved may be delivered,
Save with your right hand,
And answer us.

REFRAIN
Peace among men in whom he is well pleased.

THE LORD'S PRAYER
Our Father in heaven,
Hallowed be your name.
Your kingdom come.
Your will be done,
On earth as it is in heaven.
Give us this day our daily bread.
Forgive us our debts, as we forgive our debtors.
Lead us not into temptation,
But deliver us from the evil one.
For yours is the kingdom and the power and the glory
Forever and ever.

SHEMA & THE JESUS CREED
Hear, O Israel:
The Lord is our God, the Lord alone. You shall love the Lord your God with all your heart, and with all your soul and with all your might. You shall love your neighbor as yourself. There is no commandment greater than these.

CLOSING
We say yes! Amen!
Come Lord Jesus.

DAY 26
NOON
—

REFRAIN
Peace among men in whom he is well pleased.

† SILENCE

THE LORD'S PRAYER
Our Father in heaven,
Hallowed be your name.
Your kingdom come.

Your will be done,
On earth as it is in heaven.
Give us this day our daily bread.
Forgive us our debts, as we forgive our debtors.
Lead us not into temptation,
But deliver us from the evil one.
For yours is the kingdom and the power and the glory
Forever and ever.

SHEMA & THE JESUS CREED
Hear, O Israel:
The Lord is our God, the Lord alone. You shall love the Lord your God with all your heart, and with all your soul and with all your might. You shall love your neighbor as yourself. There is no commandment greater than these.

CLOSING
We say yes! Amen!
Come Lord Jesus.

DAY 26
EVENING
—

REFRAIN
Peace among men in whom he is well pleased.

† SILENCE

GLORIA
Peace among men in whom he is well pleased.

The shining glory of the Lord
All around.
Do not be afraid.
Behold,
Good tidings of great joy
To all the people.
There is born to us
In the city of David

A Savior, who is Christ the Lord.

Peace among men in whom he is well pleased.

Glory to God in the highest heavens,
And on earth peace
Among men in whom he is well pleased.

† SILENCE

REFRAIN
Peace among men in whom he is well pleased.

PSALM 127
Unless Yahweh builds the house,
They labor in vain that build it:
Unless Yahweh keeps the city,
The watchman wake in vain.
It is vain for you to rise up early,
To take rest late,
To eat the bread of toil;
For he gives unto his beloved as they sleep.

REFRAIN
Peace among men in whom he is well pleased.

THE LORD'S PRAYER
Our Father in heaven,
Hallowed be your name.
Your kingdom come.
Your will be done,
On earth as it is in heaven.
Give us this day our daily bread.
Forgive us our debts, as we forgive our debtors.
Lead us not into temptation,
But deliver us from the evil one.
For yours is the kingdom and the power and the glory
Forever and ever.

SHEMA & THE JESUS CREED
Hear, O Israel:
The Lord is our God, the Lord alone. You shall love the Lord your God with all your heart, and with all your soul and with all your might. You shall love your neighbor as yourself. There is no commandment greater than these.

CLOSING
We say yes! Amen!
Come Lord Jesus.

DAY 27
MORNING
—

REFRAIN
There is born to us.

† SILENCE

GLORIA
The shining glory of the Lord
All around.
Do not be afraid.
Behold,
Good tidings of great joy
To all the people.
There is born to us
In the city of David
A Savior, who is Christ the Lord.
Glory to God in the highest heavens,
And on earth peace
Among men in whom he is well pleased.

† SILENCE

REFRAIN
There is born to us.

PSALM 85
Show us your lovingkindness,
O Yahweh,
And grant us your salvation.
I will hear what God Yahweh will speak;
For he will speak peace
Unto his people, and to his saints:
But let them not turn again to folly.
Surely his salvation is near
Those who fear him,
That glory may dwell in our land.
Mercy and truth are met together;
Righteousness and peace

Have kissed each other.
Truth springs out of the earth;
And righteousness has looked down from heaven.

REFRAIN
There is born to us.

THE LORD'S PRAYER
Our Father in heaven,
Hallowed be your name.
Your kingdom come.
Your will be done,
On earth as it is in heaven.
Give us this day our daily bread.
Forgive us our debts, as we forgive our debtors.
Lead us not into temptation,
But deliver us from the evil one.
For yours is the kingdom and the power and the glory
Forever and ever.

SHEMA & THE JESUS CREED
Hear, O Israel:
The Lord is our God, the Lord alone. You shall love the Lord your God with all your heart, and with all your soul and with all your might. You shall love your neighbor as yourself. There is no commandment greater than these.

CLOSING
We say yes! Amen!
Come Lord Jesus.

DAY 27
NOON

—

REFRAIN
There is born to us.

† SILENCE

THE LORD'S PRAYER
Our Father in heaven,
Hallowed be your name.
Your kingdom come.
Your will be done,
On earth as it is in heaven.
Give us this day our daily bread.
Forgive us our debts, as we forgive our debtors.
Lead us not into temptation,
But deliver us from the evil one.
For yours is the kingdom and the power and the glory
Forever and ever.

SHEMA & THE JESUS CREED
Hear, O Israel:
The Lord is our God, the Lord alone. You shall love the Lord your God with all your heart, and with all your soul and with all your might. You shall love your neighbor as yourself. There is no commandment greater than these.

CLOSING
We say yes! Amen!
Come Lord Jesus.

DAY 27
EVENING
—

REFRAIN
There is born to us.

† SILENCE

GLORIA
There is born to us.

The shining glory of the Lord
All around.
Do not be afraid.
Behold,

Good tidings of great joy
To all the people.
There is born to us
In the city of David
A Savior, who is Christ the Lord.

There is born to us.

Glory to God in the highest heavens,
And on earth peace
Among men in whom he is well pleased.

There is born to us.

† SILENCE

REFRAIN
There is born to us.

PSALM 130
I wait for Yahweh,
My soul does wait,
And in his word do I hope.
My soul waits for the Lord
More than watchmen
Wait for the morning;
More than watchmen for the morning.
O Israel, hope in Yahweh;
For with Yahweh there is lovingkindness,
And with him is plenteous redemption.
And he will redeem Israel
From all his iniquities.

REFRAIN
There is born to us.

THE LORD'S PRAYER
Our Father in heaven,
Hallowed be your name.
Your kingdom come.

Your will be done,
On earth as it is in heaven.
Give us this day our daily bread.
Forgive us our debts, as we forgive our debtors.
Lead us not into temptation,
But deliver us from the evil one.
For yours is the kingdom and the power and the glory
Forever and ever.

SHEMA & THE JESUS CREED
Hear, O Israel:
The Lord is our God, the Lord alone. You shall love the Lord your God with all your heart, and with all your soul and with all your might. You shall love your neighbor as yourself. There is no commandment greater than these.

CLOSING
We say yes! Amen!
Come Lord Jesus.

DAY 28
MORNING
—

REFRAIN
A Savior, who is Christ the Lord.

† SILENCE

GLORIA
The shining glory of the Lord
All around.
Do not be afraid.
Behold,
Good tidings of great joy
To all the people.
There is born to us
In the city of David
A Savior, who is Christ the Lord.
Glory to God in the highest heavens,
And on earth peace
Among men in whom he is well pleased.

† SILENCE

REFRAIN
A Savior, who is Christ the Lord.

PSALM 119
For ever, O Yahweh,
Your word is settled in heaven.
Your faithfulness
Is unto all generations:
You have established the earth,
And it abides.
They abide this day
According to your ordinances;
For all things are your servants.
Unless your law had been my delight,
I should then have perished
In my affliction.

I will never forget your precepts;
For with them
You have quickened me.
I am yours, save me.

REFRAIN
A Savior, who is Christ the Lord.

THE LORD'S PRAYER
Our Father in heaven,
Hallowed be your name.
Your kingdom come.
Your will be done,
On earth as it is in heaven.
Give us this day our daily bread.
Forgive us our debts, as we forgive our debtors.
Lead us not into temptation,
But deliver us from the evil one.
For yours is the kingdom and the power and the glory
Forever and ever.

SHEMA & THE JESUS CREED
Hear, O Israel:
The Lord is our God, the Lord alone. You shall love the Lord your God with all your heart, and with all your soul and with all your might. You shall love your neighbor as yourself. There is no commandment greater than these.

CLOSING
We say yes! Amen!
Come Lord Jesus.

DAY 28
NOON

REFRAIN
A Savior, who is Christ the Lord.

† SILENCE

THE LORD'S PRAYER
Our Father in heaven,
Hallowed be your name.
Your kingdom come.
Your will be done,
On earth as it is in heaven.
Give us this day our daily bread.
Forgive us our debts, as we forgive our debtors.
Lead us not into temptation,
But deliver us from the evil one.
For yours is the kingdom and the power and the glory
Forever and ever.

SHEMA & THE JESUS CREED
Hear, O Israel:
The Lord is our God, the Lord alone. You shall love the Lord your God with all your heart, and with all your soul and with all your might. You shall love your neighbor as yourself. There is no commandment greater than these.

CLOSING
We say yes! Amen!
Come Lord Jesus.

DAY 28
EVENING
—

REFRAIN
A Savior, who is Christ the Lord.

† SILENCE

GLORIA
A Savior, who is Christ the Lord.

The shining glory of the Lord
All around.
Do not be afraid.
Behold,

Good tidings of great joy
To all the people.
There is born to us
In the city of David
A Savior, who is Christ the Lord.

A Savior, who is Christ the Lord.

Glory to God in the highest heavens,
And on earth peace
Among men in whom he is well pleased.

A Savior, who is Christ the Lord.

† SILENCE

REFRAIN
A Savior, who is Christ the Lord.

PSALM 69
Save me, O God;
For the waters are come in unto my soul.
I sink in deep mire,
Where there is no standing:
I am come into deep waters,
Where the floods overflow me.
I am weary with my crying;
My throat is dried:
Mine eyes fail while I wait for my God.
My prayer is unto you,
O Yahweh, in an acceptable time:
O God, in the abundance of your lovingkindness,
Answer me in the truth of your salvation.
Deliver me out of the mire,
And let me not sink.
Answer me, O Yahweh;
For your lovingkindness is good:
According to the multitude of your tender mercies
Turn towards me,
Do not hide your face.

REFRAIN
A Savior, who is Christ the Lord.

THE LORD'S PRAYER
Our Father in heaven,
Hallowed be your name.
Your kingdom come.
Your will be done,
On earth as it is in heaven.
Give us this day our daily bread.
Forgive us our debts, as we forgive our debtors.
Lead us not into temptation,
But deliver us from the evil one.
For yours is the kingdom and the power and the glory
Forever and ever.

SHEMA & THE JESUS CREED
Hear, O Israel:
The Lord is our God, the Lord alone. You shall love the Lord your God with all your heart, and with all your soul and with all your might. You shall love your neighbor as yourself. There is no commandment greater than these.

CLOSING
We say yes! Amen!
Come Lord Jesus.

A PRAYER GUIDE FOR CHRISTMASTIDE

CHRISTMAS EVE MORNING

—

REFRAIN
His name shall be called
Wonderful, Counselor, Mighty God,
Everlasting Father, Prince of Peace.

† SILENCE

GLORIA
Glory in the highest heavens to God
And on earth
Peace to all people who are favored.

HYMN OF ISAIAH
For unto us a child is born,
Unto us a son is given;
And the government shall be upon his shoulder:
And his name shall be called
Wonderful, Counselor, Mighty God,
Everlasting Father, Prince of Peace.
Of the increase of his government
And of peace there shall be no end.
I create the praise of the lips:
Peace, peace, to them far off
And those near, says Yahweh;
And I will heal them.
How beautiful upon the mountains
Are the feet of him that bring good tidings,
That publish peace,
That bring good tidings of good,
That publish salvation,
That says unto Zion,
Your God reigns!
The voice of your watchmen!
They lift up the voice,
Together do they sing;
For they shall see eye to eye,
When Yahweh returns to Zion.

Break forth into joy, sing together,
You wasted places of Jerusalem;
Yahweh has comforted his people,
He has redeemed Jerusalem.

† SILENCE

REFRAIN
His name shall be called
Wonderful, Counselor, Mighty God,
Everlasting Father, Prince of Peace.

THE LORD'S PRAYER
Our Father in heaven,
Hallowed be your name.
Your kingdom come.
Your will be done,
On earth as it is in heaven.
Give us this day our daily bread.
Forgive us our debts, as we forgive our debtors.
Lead us not into temptation,
But deliver us from the evil one.
For yours is the kingdom and the power and the glory
Forever and ever.

SHEMA & THE JESUS CREED
Hear, O Israel:
The Lord is our God, the Lord alone. You shall love the Lord your God with all your heart, and with all your soul and with all your might. You shall love your neighbor as yourself. There is no commandment greater than these.

ADORATION
Come let us adore him.

CLOSING
We say yes! Amen!
Come Lord Jesus.

CHRISTMAS EVE
NOON
—

REFRAIN
His name shall be called
Wonderful, Counselor, Mighty God,
Everlasting Father, Prince of Peace.

† SILENCE

GLORIA
Glory in the highest heavens to God
And on earth
Peace to all people who are favored.

THE LORD'S PRAYER
Our Father in heaven,
Hallowed be your name.
Your kingdom come.
Your will be done,
On earth as it is in heaven.
Give us this day our daily bread.
Forgive us our debts, as we forgive our debtors.
Lead us not into temptation,
But deliver us from the evil one.
For yours is the kingdom and the power and the glory
Forever and ever.

SHEMA & THE JESUS CREED
Hear, O Israel:
The Lord is our God, the Lord alone. You shall love the Lord your God with all your heart, and with all your soul and with all your might. You shall love your neighbor as yourself. There is no commandment greater than these.

ADORATION
Come let us adore him.

CLOSING
We say yes! Amen!
Come Lord Jesus.

CHRISTMAS EVE
EVENING
—

REFRAIN
His name shall be called
Wonderful, Counselor, Mighty God,
Everlasting Father, Prince of Peace.

† SILENCE

GLORIA
Glory in the highest heavens to God
And on earth
Peace to all people who are favored.

HYMN OF ISAIAH
For unto us a child is born,
Unto us a son is given;
And the government shall be upon his shoulder:
And his name shall be called
Wonderful, Counselor, Mighty God,
Everlasting Father, Prince of Peace.
Of the increase of his government
And of peace there shall be no end.
I create the praise of the lips:
Peace, peace, to them far off
And those near, says Yahweh;
And I will heal them.
How beautiful upon the mountains
Are the feet of him that bring good tidings,
That publish peace,
That bring good tidings of good,
That publish salvation,
That says unto Zion,
Your God reigns!

The voice of your watchmen!
They lift up the voice,
Together do they sing;
For they shall see eye to eye,
When Yahweh returns to Zion.
Break forth into joy, sing together,
You wasted places of Jerusalem;
Yahweh has comforted his people,
He has redeemed Jerusalem.

† SILENCE

REFRAIN
His name shall be called
Wonderful, Counselor, Mighty God,
Everlasting Father, Prince of Peace.

THE LORD'S PRAYER
Our Father in heaven,
Hallowed be your name.
Your kingdom come.
Your will be done,
On earth as it is in heaven.
Give us this day our daily bread.
Forgive us our debts, as we forgive our debtors.
Lead us not into temptation,
But deliver us from the evil one.
For yours is the kingdom and the power and the glory
Forever and ever.

SHEMA & THE JESUS CREED
Hear, O Israel:
The Lord is our God, the Lord alone. You shall love the Lord
your God with all your heart, and with all your soul and with all
your might. You shall love your neighbor as yourself. There is no
commandment greater than these.

ADORATION
Come let us adore him.

CLOSING
We say yes! Amen!
Come Lord Jesus.

CHRISTMAS DAY
MORNING
—

REFRAIN
The Word became flesh
And dwelt among us.

† SILENCE

GLORIA
Glory in the highest heavens to God
And on earth
Peace to all people who are favored.

LOGOS HYMN
In the beginning was the Word,
And the Word was with God,
And the Word was God.
He was in the beginning with God.
All things were made through him;
And without him nothing was made
That has been made.
In him was life;
And the life was the light of men.
The light shines in the darkness;
And the darkness has not apprehended it.
There was the true light,
The light which lights everyone,
Coming into the world.
He was in the world,
And the world was made through him,
But the world knew him not.
He came unto his own,
And his own did not receive him.
But to all who received him,
Who put their trust on his name
He gave the right to become children of God,
Born, not of blood,
Not of the will of the flesh,
Not of the will of man,

But of God.
And the Word became flesh,
And dwelt among us
And we beheld his glory,
Glory as of the only begotten from the Father,
Full of grace and truth.
No man has seen God at any time;
The only begotten Son,
Who is in the bosom of the Father,
He has declared him.
Behold, the Lamb of God,
That takes away the sin of the world!

† SILENCE

REFRAIN
The Word became flesh
And dwelt among us.

THE LORD'S PRAYER
Our Father in heaven,
Hallowed be your name.
Your kingdom come.
Your will be done,
On earth as it is in heaven
Give us this day our daily bread.
Forgive us our debts, as we forgive our debtors.
Lead us not into temptation,
But deliver us from the evil one.
For yours is the kingdom and the power and the glory
Forever and ever.

SHEMA & THE JESUS CREED
Hear, O Israel:
The Lord is our God, the Lord alone. You shall love the Lord your God with all your heart, and with all your soul and with all your might. You shall love your neighbor as yourself. There is no commandment greater than these.

CLOSING
We say yes! Amen!
Come Lord Jesus.

CHRISTMAS DAY
NOON
—

REFRAIN
The Word became flesh
And dwelt among us.

† SILENCE

GLORIA
Glory in the highest heavens to God
And on earth
Peace to all people who are favored.

THE LORD'S PRAYER
Our Father in heaven,
Hallowed be your name.
Your kingdom come.
Your will be done,
On earth as it is in heaven.
Give us this day our daily bread.
Forgive us our debts, as we forgive our debtors.
Lead us not into temptation,
But deliver us from the evil one.
For yours is the kingdom and the power and the glory
Forever and ever.

SHEMA & THE JESUS CREED
Hear, O Israel:
The Lord is our God, the Lord alone. You shall love the Lord your God with all your heart, and with all your soul and with all your might. You shall love your neighbor as yourself. There is no commandment greater than these.

CLOSING
We say yes! Amen!
Come Lord Jesus.

CHRISTMAS DAY
EVENING
—

REFRAIN
The Word became flesh
And dwelt among us.

† SILENCE

GLORIA
Glory in the highest heavens to God
And on earth
Peace to all people who are favored.

LOGOS HYMN
In the beginning was the Word,
And the Word was with God,
And the Word was God.
He was in the beginning with God.
All things were made through him;
And without him nothing was made
That has been made.
In him was life;
And the life was the light of men.
The light shines in the darkness;
And the darkness has not apprehended it.
There was the true light,
The light which lights everyone,
Coming into the world.
He was in the world,
And the world was made through him,
But the world knew him not.
He came unto his own,
And his own did not receive him.
But to all who received him,

Who put their trust on his name
He gave the right to become children of God,
Born, not of blood,
Not of the will of the flesh,
Not of the will of man,
But of God.
And the Word became flesh,
And dwelt among us
And we beheld his glory,
Glory as of the only begotten from the Father,
Full of grace and truth.
No man has seen God at any time;
The only begotten Son,
Who is in the bosom of the Father,
He has declared him.
Behold, the Lamb of God,
That takes away the sin of the world!

† SILENCE

REFRAIN
The Word became flesh
And dwelt among us.

THE LORD'S PRAYER
Our Father in heaven,
Hallowed be your name.
Your kingdom come.
Your will be done,
On earth as it is in heaven.
Give us this day our daily bread.
Forgive us our debts, as we forgive our debtors.
Lead us not into temptation,
But deliver us from the evil one.
For yours is the kingdom and the power and the glory
Forever and ever.

SHEMA & THE JESUS CREED
Hear, O Israel:
The Lord is our God, the Lord alone. You shall love the Lord

your God with all your heart, and with all your soul and with all your might. You shall love your neighbor as yourself. There is no commandment greater than these.

CLOSING
We say yes! Amen!
Come Lord Jesus.

SECOND DAY OF CHRISTMAS
MORNING
—

REFRAIN
He made himself nothing.

† SILENCE

GLORIA
Glory in the highest heavens to God
And on earth
Peace to all people who are favored.

HYMN OF PHILIPPI
Have the same mind as Christ Jesus:
Who, being in very nature God,
Did not consider equality with God
Something to be used to his own advantage;
Rather, he made himself nothing
By taking the very nature of a servant,
Being made in human likeness.
And being found in appearance as a man,
He humbled himself
By becoming obedient to death—
Even death on a cross!
Therefore God exalted him to the highest place
And gave him the name that is above every name,
That at the name of Jesus every knee should bow,
In heaven and on earth and under the earth,
And every tongue acknowledge
That Jesus Christ is Lord,
To the glory of God the Father.

† SILENCE

REFRAIN
He made himself nothing.

THE LORD'S PRAYER
Our Father in heaven,
Hallowed be your name.
Your kingdom come.
Your will be done,
On earth as it is in heaven.
Give us this day our daily bread.
Forgive us our debts, as we forgive our debtors.
Lead us not into temptation,
But deliver us from the evil one.
For yours is the kingdom and the power and the glory
Forever and ever.

SHEMA & THE JESUS CREED
Hear, O Israel:
The Lord is our God, the Lord alone. You shall love the Lord your God with all your heart, and with all your soul and with all your might. You shall love your neighbor as yourself. There is no commandment greater than these.

CLOSING
We say yes! Amen!
Come Lord Jesus.

SECOND DAY OF CHRISTMAS
NOON

—

REFRAIN
He made himself nothing.

† SILENCE

GLORIA
Glory in the highest heavens to God
And on earth
Peace to all people who are favored.

THE LORD'S PRAYER
Our Father in heaven,

Hallowed be your name.
Your kingdom come.
Your will be done,
On earth as it is in heaven.
Give us this day our daily bread.
Forgive us our debts, as we forgive our debtors.
Lead us not into temptation,
But deliver us from the evil one.
For yours is the kingdom and the power and the glory
Forever and ever.

SHEMA & THE JESUS CREED
Hear, O Israel:
The Lord is our God, the Lord alone. You shall love the Lord your God with all your heart, and with all your soul and with all your might. You shall love your neighbor as yourself. There is no commandment greater than these.

CLOSING
We say yes! Amen!
Come Lord Jesus.

SECOND DAY OF CHRISTMAS
EVENING
—

REFRAIN
He made himself nothing.

† SILENCE

GLORIA
Glory in the highest heavens to God
And on earth
Peace to all people who are favored.

HYMN OF PHILIPPI
Have the same mindset as Christ Jesus:
Who, being in very nature God,
Did not consider equality with God

Something to be used to his own advantage;
Rather, he made himself nothing
By taking the very nature of a servant,
Being made in human likeness.
And being found in appearance as a man,
He humbled himself
By becoming obedient to death—
Even death on a cross!
Therefore God exalted him to the highest place
And gave him the name that is above every name,
That at the name of Jesus every knee should bow,
In heaven and on earth and under the earth,
And every tongue acknowledge
That Jesus Christ is Lord,
To the glory of God the Father.

† SILENCE

REFRAIN
He made himself nothing.

THE LORD'S PRAYER
Our Father in heaven,
Hallowed be your name.
Your kingdom come.
Your will be done,
On earth as it is in heaven.
Give us this day our daily bread.
Forgive us our debts, as we forgive our debtors.
Lead us not into temptation,
But deliver us from the evil one.
For yours is the kingdom and the power and the glory
Forever and ever.

SHEMA & THE JESUS CREED
Hear, O Israel:
The Lord is our God, the Lord alone. You shall love the Lord your God with all your heart, and with all your soul and with all your might. You shall love your neighbor as yourself. There is no commandment greater than these.

CLOSING
We say yes! Amen!
Come Lord Jesus.

THIRD DAY OF CHRISTMAS
MORNING

REFRAIN
God sent forth the Spirit of his Son
Into our hearts,
Crying, Abba, Father.
So we are no longer slaves,
But sons and daughters.

† SILENCE

GLORIA
Glory in the highest heavens to God
And on earth
Peace to all people who are favored.

HYMN OF GALATIANS IV
When we were children
We were enslaved
To this world's elementary principals
But when the fullness of the time came,
God sent forth his Son,
Born of a woman,
Born under the law,
That he might redeem those under the law,
That we might receive the adoption of sons and daughters.
And because we are sons and daughters,
God sent forth the Spirit of his Son into our hearts,
Crying, Abba, Father.
So we are no longer slaves,
But sons and daughters;
And if sons and daughters,
Then heirs through God.
Christ be formed in us.

† SILENCE

REFRAIN
God sent forth the Spirit of his Son
Into our hearts,
Crying, Abba, Father.
So we are no longer slaves,
But sons and daughters.

THE LORD'S PRAYER
Our Father in heaven,
Hallowed be your name.
Your kingdom come.
Your will be done,
On earth as it is in heaven.
Give us this day our daily bread.
Forgive us our debts, as we forgive our debtors.
Lead us not into temptation,
But deliver us from the evil one.
For yours is the kingdom and the power and the glory
Forever and ever.

SHEMA & THE JESUS CREED
Hear, O Israel:
The Lord is our God, the Lord alone. You shall love the Lord your God with all your heart, and with all your soul and with all your might. You shall love your neighbor as yourself. There is no commandment greater than these.

CLOSING
We say yes! Amen!
Come Lord Jesus.

THIRD DAY OF CHRISTMAS
NOON

—

REFRAIN
God sent forth the Spirit of his Son
Into our hearts,

Crying, Abba, Father.
So we are no longer slaves,
But sons and daughters.

† SILENCE

GLORIA
Glory in the highest heavens to God
And on earth
Peace to all people who are favored.

THE LORD'S PRAYER
Our Father in heaven,
Hallowed be your name.
Your kingdom come.
Your will be done,
On earth as it is in heaven.
Give us this day our daily bread.
Forgive us our debts, as we forgive our debtors.
Lead us not into temptation,
But deliver us from the evil one.
For yours is the kingdom and the power and the glory
Forever and ever.

SHEMA & THE JESUS CREED
Hear, O Israel:
The Lord is our God, the Lord alone. You shall love the Lord your God with all your heart, and with all your soul and with all your might. You shall love your neighbor as yourself. There is no commandment greater than these.

CLOSING
We say yes! Amen!
Come Lord Jesus.

THIRD DAY OF CHRISTMAS
EVENING

—

REFRAIN
God sent forth the Spirit of his Son
Into our hearts,
Crying, Abba, Father.
So we are no longer slaves,
But sons and daughters.

† SILENCE

GLORIA
Glory in the highest heavens to God
And on earth
Peace to all people who are favored.

HYMN OF GALATIANS IV
When we were children
We were enslaved
To this world's elementary principals
But when the fullness of the time came,
God sent forth his Son,
Born of a woman,
Born under the law,
That he might redeem those under the law,
That we might receive the adoption of sons and daughters.
And because we are sons and daughters,
God sent forth the Spirit of his Son into our hearts,
Crying, Abba, Father.
So we are no longer slaves,
But sons and daughters;
And if sons and daughters,
Then heirs through God.
Christ be formed in us.

† SILENCE

A Prayer Guide for Advent | 175

REFRAIN
God sent forth the Spirit of his Son
Into our hearts,
Crying, Abba, Father.
So we are no longer slaves,
But sons and daughters.

THE LORD'S PRAYER
Our Father in heaven,
Hallowed be your name.
Your kingdom come.
Your will be done,
On earth as it is in heaven.
Give us this day our daily bread.
Forgive us our debts, as we forgive our debtors.
Lead us not into temptation,
But deliver us from the evil one.
For yours is the kingdom and the power and the glory
Forever and ever.

SHEMA & THE JESUS CREED
Hear, O Israel:
The Lord is our God, the Lord alone. You shall love the Lord your God with all your heart, and with all your soul and with all your might. You shall love your neighbor as yourself. There is no commandment greater than these.

CLOSING
We say yes! Amen!
Come Lord Jesus.

FOURTH DAY OF CHRISTMAS
MORNING
—

REFRAIN
But will God really dwell on the earth?

† SILENCE

GLORIA
Glory in the highest heavens to God
And on earth
Peace to all people who are favored.

HYMN OF SOLOMON
O Yahweh, the God of Israel,
There is no God like you,
In heaven above, or on earth beneath;
Who keeps his covenant and lovingkindness
With his servants that walk before you
With all their heart.
But will God really dwell on the earth?
Behold, heaven and the heaven of heavens
Cannot contain you;
How much less this house that I have built!
Yet you hear the prayer of your servant.
O Yahweh my God,
Hearken unto my cry and prayer.
Yahweh our God be with us, as he was with our fathers:
Let him not leave us, nor forsake us;
That he may incline our hearts unto him,
To walk in all his ways.

† SILENCE

REFRAIN
But will God really dwell on the earth?

THE LORD'S PRAYER
Our Father in heaven,
Hallowed be your name.

Your kingdom come.
Your will be done,
On earth as it is in heaven.
Give us this day our daily bread.
Forgive us our debts, as we forgive our debtors.
Lead us not into temptation,
But deliver us from the evil one.
For yours is the kingdom and the power and the glory
Forever and ever.

SHEMA & THE JESUS CREED
Hear, O Israel:
The Lord is our God, the Lord alone. You shall love the Lord your God with all your heart, and with all your soul and with all your might. You shall love your neighbor as yourself. There is no commandment greater than these.

CLOSING
We say yes! Amen!
Come Lord Jesus.

FOURTH DAY OF CHRISTMAS
NOON

REFRAIN
But will God really dwell on the earth?

† SILENCE

GLORIA
Glory in the highest heavens to God
And on earth
Peace to all people who are favored.

† SILENCE

REFRAIN
But will God really dwell on the earth?

THE LORD'S PRAYER
Our Father in heaven,
Hallowed be your name.
Your kingdom come.
Your will be done,
On earth as it is in heaven.
Give us this day our daily bread.
Forgive us our debts, as we forgive our debtors.
Lead us not into temptation,
But deliver us from the evil one.
For yours is the kingdom and the power and the glory
Forever and ever.

SHEMA & THE JESUS CREED
Hear, O Israel:
The Lord is our God, the Lord alone. You shall love the Lord your God with all your heart, and with all your soul and with all your might. You shall love your neighbor as yourself. There is no commandment greater than these.

CLOSING
We say yes! Amen!
Come Lord Jesus.

FOURTH DAY OF CHRISTMAS
EVENING
—

REFRAIN
But will God really dwell on the earth?

† SILENCE

GLORIA
Glory in the highest heavens to God
And on earth
Peace to all people who are favored.

† SILENCE

A Prayer Guide for Advent

HYMN OF SOLOMON
O Yahweh, the God of Israel,
There is no God like you,
In heaven above, or on earth beneath;
Who keeps his covenant and lovingkindness
With his servants that walk before you
With all their heart.
But will God really dwell on the earth?
Behold, heaven and the heaven of heavens
Cannot contain you;
How much less this house that I have built!
Yet you hear the prayer of your servant.
O Yahweh my God,
Hearken unto my cry and prayer.
Yahweh our God be with us, as he was with our fathers:
Let him not leave us, nor forsake us;
That he may incline our hearts unto him,
To walk in all his ways.

† SILENCE

REFRAIN
But will God really dwell on the earth?

THE LORD'S PRAYER
Our Father in heaven,
Hallowed be your name.
Your kingdom come.
Your will be done,
On earth as it is in heaven.
Give us this day our daily bread.
Forgive us our debts, as we forgive our debtors.
Lead us not into temptation,
But deliver us from the evil one.
For yours is the kingdom and the power and the glory
Forever and ever.

SHEMA & THE JESUS CREED
Hear, O Israel:
The Lord is our God, the Lord alone. You shall love the Lord

your God with all your heart, and with all your soul and with all your might. You shall love your neighbor as yourself. There is no commandment greater than these.

CLOSING
We say yes! Amen!
Come Lord Jesus.

FIFTH DAY OF CHRISTMAS
MORNING

—

REFRAIN
The fullness of him fills all in all.

† SILENCE

GLORIA
Glory in the highest heavens to God
And on earth
Peace to all people who are favored.

HYMN OF EPHESUS
Let the God of our Lord Jesus Christ,
The Glorious Father,
Give us the Spirit of wisdom and revelation,
So that we may know him better.
Let the eyes of our hearts be enlightened
In order that we may know
The hope to which he has called us,
The riches of his glorious inheritance
In his holy people,
And his incomparably great power
For us who believe.
The fullness of him fills all in all.
He made us alive, when we were dead.

† SILENCE

REFRAIN
The fullness of him fills all in all.

THE LORD'S PRAYER
Our Father in heaven,
Hallowed be your name.
Your kingdom come.
Your will be done,
On earth as it is in heaven.
Give us this day our daily bread.

Forgive us our debts, as we forgive our debtors.
Lead us not into temptation,
But deliver us from the evil one.
For yours is the kingdom and the power and the glory
Forever and ever.

SHEMA & THE JESUS CREED
Hear, O Israel:
The Lord is our God, the Lord alone. You shall love the Lord your God with all your heart, and with all your soul and with all your might. You shall love your neighbor as yourself. There is no commandment greater than these.

CLOSING
We say yes! Amen!
Come Lord Jesus.

FIFTH DAY OF CHRISTMAS
NOON

—

REFRAIN
The fullness of him fills all in all.

† SILENCE

GLORIA
Glory in the highest heavens to God
And on earth
Peace to all people who are favored.

THE LORD'S PRAYER
Our Father in heaven,
Hallowed be your name.
Your kingdom come.
Your will be done,
On earth as it is in heaven.
Give us this day our daily bread.
Forgive us our debts, as we forgive our debtors.
Lead us not into temptation,

But deliver us from the evil one.
For yours is the kingdom and the power and the glory
Forever and ever.

SHEMA & THE JESUS CREED
Hear, O Israel:
The Lord is our God, the Lord alone. You shall love the Lord your God with all your heart, and with all your soul and with all your might. You shall love your neighbor as yourself. There is no commandment greater than these.

CLOSING
We say yes! Amen!
Come Lord Jesus.

FIFTH DAY OF CHRISTMAS
EVENING
—

REFRAIN
The fullness of him fills all in all.

† SILENCE

GLORIA
Glory in the highest heavens to God
And on earth
Peace to all people who are favored.

HYMN OF EPHESUS
Let the God of our Lord Jesus Christ,
The glorious Father,
Give us the Spirit of wisdom and revelation,
So that we may know him better.
Let the eyes of our hearts be enlightened
In order that we may know
The hope to which he has called us,
The riches of his glorious inheritance
In his holy people,
And his incomparably great power

For us who believe.
The fullness of him fills all in all.
He made us alive, when we were dead.

† SILENCE

REFRAIN
The fullness of him fills all in all.

THE LORD'S PRAYER
Our Father in heaven,
Hallowed be your name.
Your kingdom come.
Your will be done,
On earth as it is in heaven.
Give us this day our daily bread.
Forgive us our debts, as we forgive our debtors.
Lead us not into temptation,
But deliver us from the evil one.
For yours is the kingdom and the power and the glory
Forever and ever.

SHEMA & THE JESUS CREED
Hear, O Israel:
The Lord is our God, the Lord alone. You shall love the Lord your God with all your heart, and with all your soul and with all your might. You shall love your neighbor as yourself. There is no commandment greater than these.

CLOSING
We say yes! Amen!
Come Lord Jesus.

SIXTH DAY OF CHRISTMAS
MORNING
—

REFRAIN
The kingdom of the Son of his love.

† SILENCE

GLORIA
Glory in the highest heavens to God
And on earth
Peace to all people who are favored.

HYMN OF COLOSSAE I
He delivered us out of the power of darkness,
And moved us
Into the kingdom of the Son of his love;
In whom we have our redemption,
The forgiveness of our sins.
He is the image of the invisible God,
The firstborn of all creation;
For in him were all things created,
In the heavens and upon the earth,
Things visible and things invisible,
Whether thrones, dominions, principalities or powers;
All things have been created Through him, and unto him;
He is before all things, and in him
All things consist.

† SILENCE

REFRAIN
The kingdom of the Son of his love.

THE LORD'S PRAYER
Our Father in heaven,
Hallowed be your name.
Your kingdom come.
Your will be done,
On earth as it is in heaven.

Give us this day our daily bread.
Forgive us our debts, as we forgive our debtors.
Lead us not into temptation,
But deliver us from the evil one.
For yours is the kingdom and the power and the glory
Forever and ever.

SHEMA & THE JESUS CREED
Hear, O Israel:
The Lord is our God, the Lord alone. You shall love the Lord your God with all your heart, and with all your soul and with all your might. You shall love your neighbor as yourself. There is no commandment greater than these.

CLOSING
We say yes! Amen!
Come Lord Jesus.

SIXTH DAY OF CHRISTMAS
NOON
—

REFRAIN
The kingdom of the Son of his love.

† SILENCE

GLORIA
Glory in the highest heavens to God
And on earth
Peace to all people who are favored.

THE LORD'S PRAYER
Our Father in heaven,
Hallowed be your name.
Your kingdom come.
Your will be done,
On earth as it is in heaven.
Give us this day our daily bread.
Forgive us our debts, as we forgive our debtors.

Lead us not into temptation,
But deliver us from the evil one.
For yours is the kingdom and the power and the glory
Forever and ever.

SHEMA & THE JESUS CREED
Hear, O Israel:
The Lord is our God, the Lord alone. You shall love the Lord your God with all your heart, and with all your soul and with all your might. You shall love your neighbor as yourself. There is no commandment greater than these.

CLOSING
We say yes! Amen!
Come Lord Jesus.

SIXTH DAY OF CHRISTMAS
EVENING
—

REFRAIN
The kingdom of the Son of his love.

† SILENCE

GLORIA
Glory in the highest heavens to God
And on earth
Peace to all people who are favored.

† SILENCE

HYMN OF COLOSSAE I
He delivered us out of the power of darkness,
And moved us
Into the kingdom of the Son of his love;
In whom we have our redemption,
The forgiveness of our sins.
He is the image of the invisible God,
The firstborn of all creation;

For in him were all things created,
In the heavens and upon the earth,
Things visible and things invisible,
Whether thrones, dominions, principalities or powers;
All things have been created Through him, and unto him;
He is before all things, and in him
All things consist.

† SILENCE

REFRAIN
The kingdom of the Son of his love.

THE LORD'S PRAYER
Our Father in heaven,
Hallowed be your name.
Your kingdom come.
Your will be done,
On earth as it is in heaven.
Give us this day our daily bread.
Forgive us our debts, as we forgive our debtors.
Lead us not into temptation,
But deliver us from the evil one.
For yours is the kingdom and the power and the glory
Forever and ever.

SHEMA & THE JESUS CREED
Hear, O Israel:
The Lord is our God, the Lord alone. You shall love the Lord your God with all your heart, and with all your soul and with all your might. You shall love your neighbor as yourself. There is no commandment greater than these.

CLOSING
We say yes! Amen!
Come Lord Jesus.

SEVENTH DAY OF CHRISTMAS
MORNING

—

REFRAIN
In Christ all the fullness dwells.

† SILENCE

GLORIA
Glory in the highest heavens to God
And on earth
Peace to all people who are favored.

HYMN OF COLOSSAE II
All things have been created through him,
And unto him;
And he is before all things,
And in him all things consist.
And he is the head of the body, the church:
He is the beginning,
The firstborn from the dead;
That in all things
He might have the preeminence.
For it was the good pleasure of the Father
That in him should all the fullness dwell;
And through him
To reconcile all things unto himself,
Having made peace
Through the blood of his cross;
Things upon the earth,
Or things in the heavens.
May your hearts be comforted,
May they being knit together in love,
May they know the mystery of God,
Christ,
In whom are hidden
All the treasures of wisdom and knowledge.

† SILENCE

REFRAIN
In Christ all the fullness dwells.

THE LORD'S PRAYER
Our Father in heaven,
Hallowed be your name.
Your kingdom come.
Your will be done,
On earth as it is in heaven.
Give us this day our daily bread.
Forgive us our debts, as we forgive our debtors.
Lead us not into temptation,
But deliver us from the evil one.
For yours is the kingdom and the power and the glory
Forever and ever.

SHEMA & THE JESUS CREED
Hear, O Israel:
The Lord is our God, the Lord alone. You shall love the Lord your God with all your heart, and with all your soul and with all your might. You shall love your neighbor as yourself. There is no commandment greater than these.

CLOSING
We say yes! Amen!
Come Lord Jesus.

SEVENTH DAY OF CHRISTMAS
NOON
—

REFRAIN
In Christ all the fullness dwells.

† **SILENCE**

GLORIA
Glory in the highest heavens to God
And on earth
Peace to all people who are favored.

A Prayer Guide for Advent

THE LORD'S PRAYER
Our Father in heaven,
Hallowed be your name.
Your kingdom come.
Your will be done,
On earth as it is in heaven.
Give us this day our daily bread.
Forgive us our debts, as we forgive our debtors.
Lead us not into temptation,
But deliver us from the evil one.
For yours is the kingdom and the power and the glory
Forever and ever.

SHEMA & THE JESUS CREED
Hear, O Israel:
The Lord is our God, the Lord alone. You shall love the Lord your God with all your heart, and with all your soul and with all your might. You shall love your neighbor as yourself. There is no commandment greater than these.

CLOSING
We say yes! Amen!
Come Lord Jesus.

SEVENTH DAY OF CHRISTMAS
EVENING
—

REFRAIN
In Christ all the fullness dwells.

† SILENCE

GLORIA
Glory in the highest heavens to God
And on earth
Peace to all people who are favored.

HYMN OF COLOSSAE II
All things have been created through him,

And unto him;
And he is before all things,
And in him all things consist.
And he is the head of the body, the church:
He is the beginning,
The firstborn from the dead;
That in all things
He might have the preeminence.
For it was the good pleasure of the Father
That in him should all the fullness dwell;
And through him
To reconcile all things unto himself,
Having made peace
Through the blood of his cross;
Things upon the earth,
Or things in the heavens.
May your hearts be comforted,
May they being knit together in love,
May they know the mystery of God,
Christ,
In whom are hidden
All the treasures of wisdom and knowledge.

† SILENCE

REFRAIN
In Christ all the fullness dwells.

THE LORD'S PRAYER
Our Father in heaven,
Hallowed be your name.
Your kingdom come.
Your will be done,
On earth as it is in heaven.
Give us this day our daily bread.
Forgive us our debts, as we forgive our debtors.
Lead us not into temptation,
But deliver us from the evil one.
For yours is the kingdom and the power and the glory
Forever and ever.

SHEMA & THE JESUS CREED
Hear, O Israel:
The Lord is our God, the Lord alone. You shall love the Lord your God with all your heart, and with all your soul and with all your might. You shall love your neighbor as yourself. There is no commandment greater than these.

CLOSING
We say yes! Amen!
Come Lord Jesus.

EIGHTH DAY OF CHRISTMAS
MORNING

—

REFRAIN
Jesus Christ, the radiance of God's glory.

† SILENCE

GLORIA
Glory in the highest heavens to God
And on earth
Peace to all people who are favored.

HYMN OF HEBREWS
At many times and in many ways
Long ago
God spoke to our fathers by the prophets.
In these last days he has spoken in his Son.
Whom he appointed heir of all things,
Through whom also he made the worlds;
Who being the radiance of his glory,
And the exact representation of his nature,
And upholding all things
By the word of his power,
When he had made purification of sins,
Sat down on the right hand
Of the Majesty on high;
Having become by so much greater than the angels,
As he has inherited a more excellent name than them.
For unto which of the angels has God said at any time,
You are my Son,
This day have I begotten you?
And again,
I will be to him a Father,
And he shall be to me a Son?

† SILENCE

REFRAIN
Jesus Christ, the radiance of God's glory.

THE LORD'S PRAYER

Our Father in heaven,
Hallowed be your name.
Your kingdom come.
Your will be done,
On earth as it is in heaven.
Give us this day our daily bread.
Forgive us our debts, as we forgive our debtors.
Lead us not into temptation,
But deliver us from the evil one.
For yours is the kingdom and the power and the glory
Forever and ever.

SHEMA & THE JESUS CREED

Hear, O Israel:
The Lord is our God, the Lord alone. You shall love the Lord your God with all your heart, and with all your soul and with all your might. You shall love your neighbor as yourself. There is no commandment greater than these.

CLOSING

We say yes! Amen!
Come Lord Jesus.

EIGHTH DAY OF CHRISTMAS
NOON

REFRAIN

Jesus Christ, the radiance of God's glory.

† SILENCE

GLORIA

Glory in the highest heavens to God
And on earth
Peace to all people who are favored.

THE LORD'S PRAYER
Our Father in heaven,
Hallowed be your name.
Your kingdom come.
Your will be done,
On earth as it is in heaven.
Give us this day our daily bread.
Forgive us our debts, as we forgive our debtors.
Lead us not into temptation,
But deliver us from the evil one.
For yours is the kingdom and the power and the glory
Forever and ever.

SHEMA & THE JESUS CREED
Hear, O Israel:
The Lord is our God, the Lord alone. You shall love the Lord your God with all your heart, and with all your soul and with all your might. You shall love your neighbor as yourself. There is no commandment greater than these.

CLOSING
We say yes! Amen!
Come Lord Jesus.

EIGHTH DAY OF CHRISTMAS
EVENING

—

REFRAIN
Jesus Christ, the radiance of God's glory.

† SILENCE

GLORIA
Glory in the highest heavens to God
And on earth
Peace to all people who are favored.

HYMN OF HEBREWS

At many times and in many ways
Long ago
God spoke to our fathers by the prophets.
In these last days he has spoken in his Son.
Whom he appointed heir of all things,
Through whom also he made the worlds;
Who being the radiance of his glory,
And the exact representation of his nature,
And upholding all things
By the word of his power,
When he had made purification of sins,
Sat down on the right hand
Of the Majesty on high;
Having become by so much greater than the angels,
As he has inherited a more excellent name than them.
For unto which of the angels has God said at any time,
You are my Son,
This day have I begotten you?
And again,
I will be to him a Father,
And he shall be to me a Son?

† SILENCE

REFRAIN
Jesus Christ, the radiance of God's glory.

THE LORD'S PRAYER
Our Father in heaven,
Hallowed be your name.
Your kingdom come.
Your will be done,
On earth as it is in heaven.
Give us this day our daily bread.
Forgive us our debts, as we forgive our debtors.
Lead us not into temptation,
But deliver us from the evil one.
For yours is the kingdom and the power and the glory
Forever and ever.

SHEMA & THE JESUS CREED

Hear, O Israel:
The Lord is our God, the Lord alone. You shall love the Lord your God with all your heart, and with all your soul and with all your might. You shall love your neighbor as yourself. There is no commandment greater than these.

CLOSING

We say yes! Amen!
Come Lord Jesus.

NINTH DAY OF CHRISTMAS
MORNING

—

REFRAIN
Comfort, comfort my people,
Says your God.
Speak to the heart of Jerusalem.

† SILENCE

GLORIA
Glory in the highest heavens to God
And on earth
Peace to all people who are favored.

HYMN OF ISAIAH 40
Comfort, comfort my people,
Says your God.
Speak to the heart of Jerusalem;
And cry unto her,
That her warfare is accomplished,
That her iniquity is pardoned,
That she has received of Yahweh's hand
Double for all her sins.
The voice of one that cries,
Prepare in the wilderness
The way of Yahweh;
Make level in the desert
A highway for our God.
Every valley shall be exalted,
Every mountain and hill shall be made low;
The uneven shall be made level,
The rough places a plain:
The glory of Yahweh shall be revealed,
And all flesh shall see it together;
For the mouth of Yahweh has spoken it.
You who bear good tidings to Zion,
Get up on a high mountain;
You who bear good tidings to Jerusalem,
Lift up your voice with strength;

Lift it up, be not afraid;
Say unto the cities of Judah,
Behold, your God!
Behold, the Lord!
Yahweh will come as a mighty one,
And his arm will rule for him:
Behold, his reward is with him,
And his recompense before him.
He will feed his flock like a shepherd,
He will gather the lambs in his arm,
And carry them in his bosom,
And will gently lead
Those that have their young.

† SILENCE

REFRAIN
Comfort, comfort my people,
Says your God.
Speak to the heart of Jerusalem.

THE LORD'S PRAYER
Our Father in heaven,
Hallowed be your name.
Your kingdom come.
Your will be done,
On earth as it is in heaven.
Give us this day our daily bread.
Forgive us our debts, as we forgive our debtors.
Lead us not into temptation,
But deliver us from the evil one.
For yours is the kingdom and the power and the glory
Forever and ever.

SHEMA & THE JESUS CREED
Hear, O Israel:
The Lord is our God, the Lord alone. You shall love the Lord
your God with all your heart, and with all your soul and with all
your might. You shall love your neighbor as yourself. There is no
commandment greater than these.

CLOSING
We say yes! Amen!
Come Lord Jesus.

NINTH DAY OF CHRISTMAS
NOON
—

REFRAIN
Comfort, comfort my people,
Says your God.
Speak to the heart of Jerusalem.

† SILENCE

GLORIA
Glory in the highest heavens to God
And on earth
Peace to all people who are favored.

THE LORD'S PRAYER
Our Father in heaven,
Hallowed be your name.
Your kingdom come.
Your will be done,
On earth as it is in heaven.
Give us this day our daily bread.
Forgive us our debts, as we forgive our debtors.
Lead us not into temptation,
But deliver us from the evil one.
For yours is the kingdom and the power and the glory
Forever and ever.

SHEMA & THE JESUS CREED
Hear, O Israel:
The Lord is our God, the Lord alone. You shall love the Lord your God with all your heart, and with all your soul and with all your might. You shall love your neighbor as yourself. There is no commandment greater than these.

CLOSING
We say yes! Amen!
Come Lord Jesus.

NINTH DAY OF CHRISTMAS
EVENING
—

REFRAIN
Comfort, comfort my people,
Says your God.
Speak to the heart of Jerusalem.

† SILENCE

GLORIA
Glory in the highest heavens to God
And on earth
Peace to all people who are favored.

HYMN OF ISAIAH 40
Comfort, comfort my people,
Says your God.
Speak to the heart of Jerusalem;
And cry unto her,
That her warfare is accomplished,
That her iniquity is pardoned,
That she has received of Yahweh's hand
Double for all her sins.
The voice of one that cries,
Prepare in the wilderness
The way of Yahweh;
Make level in the desert
A highway for our God.
Every valley shall be exalted,
Every mountain and hill shall be made low;
The uneven shall be made level,
The rough places a plain:
The glory of Yahweh shall be revealed,
And all flesh shall see it together;

For the mouth of Yahweh has spoken it.
You who bear good tidings to Zion,
Get up on a high mountain;
You who bear good tidings to Jerusalem,
Lift up your voice with strength;
Lift it up, be not afraid;
Say unto the cities of Judah,
Behold, your God!
Behold, the Lord!
Yahweh will come as a mighty one,
And his arm will rule for him:
Behold, his reward is with him,
And his recompense before him.
He will feed his flock like a shepherd,
He will gather the lambs in his arm,
And carry them in his bosom,
And will gently lead
Those that have their young.

† SILENCE

REFRAIN
Comfort, comfort my people,
Says your God.
Speak to the heart of Jerusalem.

THE LORD'S PRAYER
Our Father in heaven,
Hallowed be your name.
Your kingdom come.
Your will be done,
On earth as it is in heaven.
Give us this day our daily bread.
Forgive us our debts, as we forgive our debtors.
Lead us not into temptation,
But deliver us from the evil one.
For yours is the kingdom and the power and the glory
Forever and ever.

SHEMA & THE JESUS CREED

Hear, O Israel:
The Lord is our God, the Lord alone. You shall love the Lord your God with all your heart, and with all your soul and with all your might. You shall love your neighbor as yourself. There is no commandment greater than these.

CLOSING

We say yes! Amen!
Come Lord Jesus.

TENTH DAY OF CHRISTMAS
MORNING
—

REFRAIN
Yea, I have loved you
With an everlasting love:
Therefore with lovingkindness have I drawn you.

† SILENCE

GLORIA
Glory in the highest heavens to God
And on earth
Peace to all people who are favored.

HYMN OF JEREMIAH 31
Yea, I have loved you
With an everlasting love:
Therefore with lovingkindness have I drawn you.
Again I will build you, you shall be rebuilt,
Arise, and let us go up to Zion
Unto Yahweh our God.
This is what Yahweh says,
Sing with gladness for Jacob,
Publish praise and say,
O Yahweh, save your people,
The remnant of Israel.
I will turn their mourning into joy,
And will comfort them,
And make them rejoice from their sorrow.
And I will satiate the soul of the priests with fatness,
And my people shall be satisfied
With my goodness.
Behold, the days come, says Yahweh,
That I will make a new covenant with the house of Israel,
I will put my law in their inward parts,
And in their heart I will write it.
I will be their God, and they shall be my people.
And they shall no longer teach
Their neighbor or brother,

Saying, know Yahweh;
For they shall all know me,
From the least of them
Unto the greatest of them.
I will forgive their iniquity,
And their sin will I remember no more.

† SILENCE

REFRAIN
Yea, I have loved you
With an everlasting love:
Therefore with lovingkindness have I drawn you.

THE LORD'S PRAYER
Our Father in heaven,
Hallowed be your name.
Your kingdom come.
Your will be done,
On earth as it is in heaven.
Give us this day our daily bread.
Forgive us our debts, as we forgive our debtors.
Lead us not into temptation,
But deliver us from the evil one.
For yours is the kingdom and the power and the glory
Forever and ever.

SHEMA & THE JESUS CREED
Hear, O Israel:
The Lord is our God, the Lord alone. You shall love the Lord your God with all your heart, and with all your soul and with all your might. You shall love your neighbor as yourself. There is no commandment greater than these.

CLOSING
We say yes! Amen!
Come Lord Jesus.

TENTH DAY OF CHRISTMAS
NOON

REFRAIN
Yea, I have loved you
With an everlasting love:
Therefore with lovingkindness have I drawn you.

† SILENCE

GLORIA
Glory in the highest heavens to God
And on earth
Peace to all people who are favored.

THE LORD'S PRAYER
Our Father in heaven,
Hallowed be your name.
Your kingdom come.
Your will be done,
On earth as it is in heaven.
Give us this day our daily bread.
Forgive us our debts, as we forgive our debtors.
Lead us not into temptation,
But deliver us from the evil one.
For yours is the kingdom and the power and the glory
Forever and ever.

SHEMA & THE JESUS CREED
Hear, O Israel:
The Lord is our God, the Lord alone. You shall love the Lord
your God with all your heart, and with all your soul and with all
your might. You shall love your neighbor as yourself. There is no
commandment greater than these.

CLOSING
We say yes! Amen!
Come Lord Jesus.

TENTH DAY OF CHRISTMAS
EVENING

—

REFRAIN
Yea, I have loved you
With an everlasting love:
Therefore with lovingkindness have I drawn you.

† SILENCE

GLORIA
Glory in the highest heavens to God
And on earth
Peace to all people who are favored.

† SILENCE

HYMN OF JEREMIAH 31
Yea, I have loved you
With an everlasting love:
Therefore with lovingkindness have I drawn you.
Again I will build you, you shall be rebuilt,
Arise, and let us go up to Zion
Unto Yahweh our God.
This is what Yahweh says,
Sing with gladness for Jacob,
Publish praise and say,
O Yahweh, save your people,
The remnant of Israel.
I will turn their mourning into joy,
And will comfort them,
And make them rejoice from their sorrow.
And I will satiate the soul of the priests with fatness,
And my people shall be satisfied
With my goodness.
Behold, the days come, says Yahweh,
That I will make a new covenant with the house of Israel,
I will put my law in their inward parts,
And in their heart I will write it.
I will be their God, and they shall be my people.

And they shall no longer teach
Their neighbor or brother,
Saying, know Yahweh;
For they shall all know me,
From the least of them
Unto the greatest of them.
I will forgive their iniquity,
And their sin will I remember no more.

† SILENCE

REFRAIN
Yea, I have loved you
With an everlasting love:
Therefore with lovingkindness have I drawn you.

THE LORD'S PRAYER
Our Father in heaven,
Hallowed be your name.
Your kingdom come.
Your will be done,
On earth as it is in heaven.
Give us this day our daily bread.
Forgive us our debts, as we forgive our debtors.
Lead us not into temptation,
But deliver us from the evil one.
For yours is the kingdom and the power and the glory
Forever and ever.

SHEMA & THE JESUS CREED
Hear, O Israel:
The Lord is our God, the Lord alone. You shall love the Lord your God with all your heart, and with all your soul and with all your might. You shall love your neighbor as yourself. There is no commandment greater than these.

CLOSING
We say yes! Amen!
Come Lord Jesus.

ELEVENTH DAY OF CHRISTMAS
MORNING
—

REFRAIN
But who can abide the day of his coming?
And who shall stand when he appears?

† SILENCE

GLORIA
Glory in the highest heavens to God
And on earth
Peace to all people who are favored.

HYMN OF MALACHI
Behold, I send my messenger,
And he shall prepare the way before me:
The Lord, whom you seek,
Will suddenly come to his temple;
The messenger of the covenant,
Whom you desire,
Behold, he comes, says Yahweh of hosts.
But who can abide the day of his coming?
And who shall stand when he appears?
For he is like a refiner's fire!
And like fullers' soap!
And he will sit as a refiner
And purifier of silver,
He will purify the sons of Levi,
And refine them as gold and silver;
And they shall offer unto Yahweh
Offerings in righteousness.
Return unto me,
And I will return unto you,
Says Yahweh of hosts.

† SILENCE

REFRAIN
But who can abide the day of his coming?
And who shall stand when he appears?

THE LORD'S PRAYER
Our Father in heaven,
Hallowed be your name.
Your kingdom come.
Your will be done,
On earth as it is in heaven.
Give us this day our daily bread.
Forgive us our debts, as we forgive our debtors.
Lead us not into temptation,
But deliver us from the evil one.
For yours is the kingdom and the power and the glory
Forever and ever.

SHEMA & THE JESUS CREED
Hear, O Israel:
The Lord is our God, the Lord alone. You shall love the Lord your God with all your heart, and with all your soul and with all your might. You shall love your neighbor as yourself. There is no commandment greater than these.

CLOSING
We say yes! Amen!
Come Lord Jesus.

ELEVENTH DAY OF CHRISTMAS
NOON
—

REFRAIN
But who can abide the day of his coming?
And who shall stand when he appears?

† SILENCE

GLORIA
Glory in the highest heavens to God
And on earth
Peace to all people who are favored.

THE LORD'S PRAYER
Our Father in heaven,
Hallowed be your name.
Your kingdom come.
Your will be done,
On earth as it is in heaven.
Give us this day our daily bread.
Forgive us our debts, as we forgive our debtors.
Lead us not into temptation,
But deliver us from the evil one.
For yours is the kingdom and the power and the glory
Forever and ever.

SHEMA & THE JESUS CREED
Hear, O Israel:
The Lord is our God, the Lord alone. You shall love the Lord your God with all your heart, and with all your soul and with all your might. You shall love your neighbor as yourself. There is no commandment greater than these.

CLOSING
We say yes! Amen!
Come Lord Jesus.

ELEVENTH DAY OF CHRISTMAS
EVENING
—

REFRAIN
But who can abide the day of his coming?
And who shall stand when he appears?

† SILENCE

GLORIA
Glory in the highest heavens to God
And on earth
Peace to all people who are favored.

HYMN OF MALACHI
Behold, I send my messenger,
And he shall prepare the way before me:
The Lord, whom you seek,
Will suddenly come to his temple;
The messenger of the covenant,
Whom you desire,
Behold, he comes, says Yahweh of hosts.
But who can abide the day of his coming?
And who shall stand when he appears?
For he is like a refiner's fire!
And like fullers' soap!
And he will sit as a refiner
And purifier of silver,
He will purify the sons of Levi,
And refine them as gold and silver;
And they shall offer unto Yahweh
Offerings in righteousness.
Return unto me,
And I will return unto you,
Says Yahweh of hosts.

† SILENCE

REFRAIN
But who can abide the day of his coming?
And who shall stand when he appears?

THE LORD'S PRAYER
Our Father in heaven,
Hallowed be your name.
Your kingdom come.
Your will be done,
On earth as it is in heaven.
Give us this day our daily bread.

Forgive us our debts, as we forgive our debtors.
Lead us not into temptation,
But deliver us from the evil one.
For yours is the kingdom and the power and the glory
Forever and ever.

SHEMA & THE JESUS CREED
Hear, O Israel:
The Lord is our God, the Lord alone. You shall love the Lord your God with all your heart, and with all your soul and with all your might. You shall love your neighbor as yourself. There is no commandment greater than these.

CLOSING
We say yes! Amen!
Come Lord Jesus.

TWELFTH DAY OF CHRISTMAS
MORNING
—

REFRAIN
For Yahweh, even Yahweh,
Is my strength and song;
And he is become my salvation.

† SILENCE

GLORIA
Glory in the highest heavens to God
And on earth
Peace to all people who are favored.

HYMN OF ISAIAH 11
And there shall come forth a shoot
Out of the stem of Jesse,
And a branch out of his roots shall bear fruit.
And the Spirit of Yahweh shall rest upon him,
The spirit of wisdom and understanding,
The spirit of counsel and might,
The spirit of knowledge and of the reverence of Yahweh.
And his delight shall be in the reverence of Yahweh;
And he shall not judge after what his eyes see,
Nor decide after what his ears hear;
But with righteousness shall he judge the poor,
And decide with equity for the meek of the earth;
And he shall smite the earth with the rod of his mouth;
And with the breath of his lips shall he slay the wicked.
And righteousness shall be the belt about his waist,
And faithfulness the belt of his loins.
And the wolf shall dwell with the lamb,
And the leopard shall lie down with the kid;
And the calf and the young lion and the fatling together;
And a little child shall lead them.
And the cow and the bear shall graze;
Their young ones shall lie down together;
And the lion shall eat straw like the ox.
And the sucking child shall play on the hole of the asp,

And the weaned child shall put his hand on the adder's den.
They shall not hurt nor destroy in all my holy mountain;
For the earth shall be full of the knowledge of Yahweh,
As the waters cover the sea.
And it shall come to pass in that day,
That the root of Jesse,
That stands for the peoples,
Unto him the nations shall seek;
And his resting place shall be glorious.
And in that day we shall say,
I will give thanks unto you,
O Yahweh;
For though you were angry with me,
Your anger is turned away
And you have comforted me.
Behold, God is my salvation;
I will trust, and will not be afraid;
For Yahweh, even Yahweh, is my strength and song;
And he is become my salvation.

† SILENCE

REFRAIN
For Yahweh, even Yahweh,
Is my strength and song;
And he is become my salvation.

THE LORD'S PRAYER
Our Father in heaven,
Hallowed be your name.
Your kingdom come.
Your will be done,
On earth as it is in heaven.
Give us this day our daily bread.
Forgive us our debts, as we forgive our debtors.
Lead us not into temptation,
But deliver us from the evil one.
For yours is the kingdom and the power and the glory
Forever and ever.

A Prayer Guide for Advent

SHEMA & THE JESUS CREED
Hear, O Israel:
The Lord is our God, the Lord alone. You shall love the Lord your God with all your heart, and with all your soul and with all your might. You shall love your neighbor as yourself. There is no commandment greater than these.

CLOSING
We say yes! Amen!
Come Lord Jesus.

TWELFTH DAY OF CHRISTMAS
NOON

REFRAIN
For Yahweh, even Yahweh,
Is my strength and song;
And he is become my salvation.

† SILENCE

GLORIA
Glory in the highest heavens to God
And on earth
Peace to all people who are favored.

THE LORD'S PRAYER
Our Father in heaven,
Hallowed be your name.
Your kingdom come.
Your will be done,
On earth as it is in heaven.
Give us this day our daily bread.
Forgive us our debts, as we forgive our debtors.
Lead us not into temptation,
But deliver us from the evil one.
For yours is the kingdom and the power and the glory
Forever and ever.

SHEMA & THE JESUS CREED
Hear, O Israel:
The Lord is our God, the Lord alone. You shall love the Lord your God with all your heart, and with all your soul and with all your might. You shall love your neighbor as yourself. There is no commandment greater than these.

CLOSING
We say yes! Amen!
Come Lord Jesus.

TWELFTH DAY OF CHRISTMAS
EVENING
—

REFRAIN
For Yahweh, even Yahweh,
Is my strength and song;
And he is become my salvation.

† SILENCE

GLORIA
Glory in the highest heavens to God
And on earth
Peace to all people who are favored.

HYMN OF ISAIAH 11
And there shall come forth a shoot
Out of the stem of Jesse,
And a branch out of his roots shall bear fruit.
And the Spirit of Yahweh shall rest upon him,
The spirit of wisdom and understanding,
The spirit of counsel and might,
The spirit of knowledge and of the reverence of Yahweh.
And his delight shall be in the reverence of Yahweh;
And he shall not judge after what his eyes see,
Nor decide after what his ears hear;
But with righteousness shall he judge the poor,
And decide with equity for the meek of the earth;

And he shall smite the earth with the rod of his mouth;
And with the breath of his lips shall he slay the wicked.
And righteousness shall be the belt about his waist,
And faithfulness the belt of his loins.
And the wolf shall dwell with the lamb,
And the leopard shall lie down with the kid;
And the calf and the young lion and the fatling together;
And a little child shall lead them.
And the cow and the bear shall graze;
Their young ones shall lie down together;
And the lion shall eat straw like the ox.
And the sucking child shall play on the hole of the asp,
And the weaned child shall put his hand on the adder's den.
They shall not hurt nor destroy in all my holy mountain;
For the earth shall be full of the knowledge of Yahweh,
As the waters cover the sea.
And it shall come to pass in that day,
That the root of Jesse,
That stands for the peoples,
Unto him the nations shall seek;
And his resting place shall be glorious.
And in that day we shall say,
I will give thanks unto you,
O Yahweh;
For though you were angry with me,
Your anger is turned away
And you have comforted me.
Behold, God is my salvation;
I will trust, and will not be afraid;
For Yahweh, even Yahweh, is my strength and song;
And he is become my salvation.

† SILENCE

REFRAIN
For Yahweh, even Yahweh, is my strength and song;
And he is become my salvation.

THE LORD'S PRAYER

Our Father in heaven,
Hallowed be your name.
Your kingdom come.
Your will be done,
On earth as it is in heaven.
Give us this day our daily bread.
Forgive us our debts, as we forgive our debtors.
Lead us not into temptation,
But deliver us from the evil one.
For yours is the kingdom and the power and the glory
Forever and ever.

SHEMA & THE JESUS CREED

Hear, O Israel:
The Lord is our God, the Lord alone. You shall love the Lord your God with all your heart, and with all your soul and with all your might. You shall love your neighbor as yourself. There is no commandment greater than these.

CLOSING

We say yes! Amen!
Come Lord Jesus.

Made in the USA
Coppell, TX
11 November 2022